PRODIGAL WORLD

HOW WE ABANDONED GOD AND SUFFERED THE CONSEQUENCES

PHILLIP D. JENSEN

Prodigal World
© Matthias Media, 2003

Matthias Media
(St Matthias Press Ltd. ACN 067 558 365)
PO Box 225
Kingsford NSW 2032 Australia
Telephone: (02) 9663 1478; Facsimile: (02) 9663 3265
International: +61-2-9663 1478; Facsimile: +61-2-9663 3265
Email: info@matthiasmedia.com.au
Internet: www.matthiasmedia.com.au

Distributed in the United Kingdom by:
The Good Book Company
Telephone: 0845-225-0880
Facsimile: 0845-225-0990
Email: admin@thegoodbook.co.uk
Internet: www.thegoodbook.co.uk

Distributed in South Africa by:
Christian Book Discounters
Telephone: (021) 685 3663
Email: peter@christianbooks.co.za

Unless otherwise indicated, all Scripture quotations are from the HOLY BIBLE, NEW INTERNATIONAL VERSION. Copyright © 1973, 1978, 1984 International Bible Society. Used by permission of Zondervan Bible Publishers.

Scripture quotations marked 'ESV' are taken from The Holy Bible, English Standard Version, copyright © 2001 by Crossway Bibles, a division of Good News Publishers. Used by permission. All rights reserved.

ISBN 1 876326 70 0

All rights reserved. Except as may be permitted by the Copyright Act, no part of this publication may be reproduced in any form or by any means without prior permission from the publisher.

Cover design and typesetting by Joy Lankshear Design Pty Ltd.

Acknowledgments

The essays in this volume first appeared in the following issues of the journal *kategoria: a critical review*:

'The problem', *kategoria*, 2003, 30.

✢

'Coming of age in controversy: Margaret Mead, Derek Freeman and intellectual leadership', *kategoria*, 1996, 2, pp. 9-22.

✢

'Saul: an unknowing prophet of doom', *kategoria*, 1998, 8, pp. 33-49.

✢

'Happiness on trial: has utilitarianism failed?', *kategoria*, 1998, 11, pp. 25-45.

✢

'Whose history of philosophy?', *kategoria*, 1997, 4, pp. 59-65.

✢

'Peace I did not find', *kategoria*, 1997, 7, pp. 65-72.

Table of Contents

Acknowledgments 3

Editor's preface 7

1. The problem 9

2. Coming of age in controversy: Margaret Mead,
   Derek Freeman and intellectual leadership 41

3. Saul: an unknowing prophet of doom 59

4. Happiness on trial: has utilitarianism failed? 83

5. Whose history of philosophy? 111

6. Peace I did not find 123

Editor's preface

*P*HILLIP JENSEN has been known for many years as a powerful Bible teacher and evangelist in his work as a chaplain at the University of New South Wales, as Rector of St Matthias Church, Centennial Park and more recently as Dean of St Andrew's Cathedral, Sydney.

He is perhaps less well-known for his social commentary. Both in his speaking and in published articles, Phillip has been a penetrating critic of the hypocrisies, falsehoods and double standards of our Western intellectual leadership. He has consistently argued that in abandoning God and Christian thought, the West has abandoned the foundations of its culture. Like the Prodigal Son of the biblical parable, we have run away from God, foolishly wasted our biblical inheritance, and now find ourselves lost, despairing and hungry. Through all strata of society, we are suffering the consequences—in our intellectual environment, in the goals set by society, in our utter loss of meaning and in breakdown of relationships.

This collection of essays helps us understand where we went wrong by looking in general terms at the problems generated by our rejection of the Christian God, and by examining specific issues (such as utilitarianism) and specific intellectual leaders (such as Margaret

Mead, John Ralston Saul and Bertrand Russell).

These essays, which first appeared in the journal *kategoria: a critical review*, form a natural collection, useful for students, academics and any thoughtful reader. If you've ever been sceptical about the claims made about life, history or morality by leading intellectuals and media spokespersons, this is the kind of thinking you need to do.

Kirsten Birkett
2003

1.
The problem

A MEMORY FROM my university days sometimes comes back to me, with a certain poignancy. I can remember being told by an earnest sociology lecturer that multiculturalism—although they used a different name for it then—was the hope for the future of the world. The idea that people could learn to live in harmony, maintaining their distinctive cultures while maintaining tolerance towards the other cultures living side-by-side, was the way forward. Assimilation was out; accepting that differences didn't really matter was in.

What were the examples of such peaceful success stories? Yugoslavia, Fiji and Ceylon (Sri Lanka).

✦

It sounds like a bad joke, now; but it's just one of the many letdowns of the twentieth century. Not that we often notice the effects. Certainly, living in Sydney as I do, it is easy to regard any shocking newspaper headlines as problems for other people. Australia is very peaceful. Generally, things are working; we have democracy, we have representation, we have (almost) free education and freedom of opinion. We do not die of starvation or rickets; food is plentiful, and the dollar stays more or less stable. Economically, we are better off than we were in past times, and than most people are in other places. We have gained enormous benefits from civilization, and can even advertise our country as a paradise—as, indeed, it sometimes seems to be.

But just occasionally, we notice with some discomfort that things are not as good as they might be. We seem to have lost the war on drugs, or at least we're losing. Alcohol abuse is costing us in serious illness, not to mention lives: the World Health Organization estimates three-quarters of a million alcohol related deaths in the world per year.[1] In Australia alone, alcohol kills more than twice as many people as road traffic accidents, and accounts for twice as many patients in drug treatment agencies as any other drug.[2]

Family and personal relationships remain vitally important for us as individuals and for the functioning of the community.[3] Nonetheless, we don't seem to be able to prevent the collapse of stable family life. If anything, it seems to be getting worse. From 1966 to 1997, the number of couple families with dependents decreased, while the number of one parent families with dependents increased; and of the couple families, an increasing percentage are de facto—which, although we may not like to think it, means that they are far more likely to be unstable.[4] Children grow up in increasingly fractured families, with no models of how to conduct a successful marriage because no one around them has one. We are a people who desperately want relationships, who desperately want something real—just read the daily newspapers, or look at the plethora of magazines offering relationship advice—but it isn't working.

It is not surprising, perhaps, that depression is increasing. The World Health Organization predicted in 1996 that by 2020 it would be the biggest health problem in the Western world, and they don't seem to be far wrong. By 1999, it was Australia's biggest cause of disability; by 2001, that conclusion was considered true worldwide.[5] At a time when we are materially better off, with less disease, less poverty, indeed with so much wealth that advertisers constantly need to invent new needs for us to spend our money on, we have never been unhappier. Contrary to all our instincts, increase in wealth does not increase our happiness.[6]

At the same time, our wealth means that we are able to be held at ransom by terrorism. The arms trade which helped to fuel the growing world economy and brought us such wealth, has now put weapons in the hands of terrorists who were once too poor to give their discontent any outlet.[7] The ethic that put increase in wealth and the power of the West above any other consideration has not only resulted in the hatred of those we abused to gain our wealth, but has also given them the means to fight back in a war we don't know how to win. The signs have been there for a long time; we're just now starting to talk seriously about them.

But what is the result of all this? We don't like the violence in the world, and we don't like violence being used to quell it, but we can't agree as to what we should do instead. In fact, we have little agreement in any ethical debate. Our technology has outstripped our ethical tools, and we can now do pretty much anything we can dream of. But so many of our dreams have turned into nightmares.

✣

In peaceful Australia—as in many other parts of the Western world—we can at times feel like we're living in paradise. But it's a brittle paradise. Living on past capital, we don't want to recognize that the problems still exist and are growing, and will only get worse. Like the rest of the Western world, we see the certainties of progress, growth, wealth and peace slipping away—and we need to understand why.

Roots of the problem

Historically and philosophically we are, in the West, Protestant. It is Protestantism that created the West—England, America, Germany, most of northern Europe, Australia. Protestantism is much more than simply being not Catholic; Protestantism is a different way of looking at the world, and in particular for our discussion here, having a different conception of how a society is organized. It means, for instance, having a particular view of the relationship of church (being the collective activities of religion) and state. It means believing that, in practice, church and state are both secular organizations—that is, they are both concerned with and operate within this temporal world. The church looks after religious affairs in the world, and the state looks after social government in the world. The state in general upholds the rule of law, and those within the church are answerable to the law, as are all citizens. It is a workable and practical system. It is different from the Catholic system, which involves quite a different view of both church and state. The Catholic view tends to identify the kingdom of God with the church, and then seeks to give the church, with all the authority of God, authority over the state. Protestants have always held these to be different things. The kingdom of God is theocratic, ruled by the authority of God; but it is not of this world. Church and state are both secular institutions, with different aims and different responsibilities; but ideally, both should conform themselves to God's wisdom, and will work best when following God's wisdom.

However the nineteenth century saw the beginnings of a shift from 'secular' to 'secular*ism*'. This was a part of a deliberate social movement with certain political and anti-church aims. The rationalist and atheist George Holyoak, for instance, coined the word 'secularism' to be a less negative-sounding alternative to 'atheism', but meaning essentially the same thing. He and other freethinkers like Charles Bradlaugh and Annie Besant worked to promote an atheistic society, consciously anti-Christian in belief and morality.[8] The secularist movement, in effect, exchanged the separation of church and state for the separation of God and state. No longer were both church and state to be secular institutions, one to run religious affairs and the other to run daily governmental affairs, both within a Christian framework; now 'secular' was defined as 'atheistic', and the state, being secular, would separate itself not just from the church but from the Christian reality behind it.

And so Western society, or at least that part of it that came to control public discourse, dispensed with God, and replaced God with man. Man, the rational machine, would run the world, which was rational, mechanistic and closed. This was not a world of miracles or metaphysics. It was a world of material, in which the answers to all questions could be discovered by human effort alone—and if they could not, then the question was meaningless or irrelevant. Romantics and spiritualists fought a rearguard action against such materialism, but like Christianity, were marginalized to the edges of respectable society.

By the twentieth century, the intellectuals of the West looked not just to a secularist (meaning atheist) society, but to a *scientific* society. The 'war' between science and religion—a war generated by the atheist rationality that sought to remove religion from respectable intellectual pursuit[9]—had been won by science. Science was the embodiment of useful, sensible, rational ways of doing things. It was time for the scientists, unfettered by superstition or reactionary emotionalism, to take over.

Lest I be accused of being just such a superstitious reactionary, I would like to praise the rise of science. Science is one of the best things to happen to the modern world, and it has been marvellously successful. Two things in particular about science stand out as worthy of praise. First, its resultant technology. Scientific research has provided us with the continued ability to manipulate the material universe and master its forces. It has given us tremendous power, much of which has been used for good. It has given ability to understand, build, create, and protect, and billions of humans have benefited from the achievements science has made possible.

Secondly, science is praiseworthy in the honesty of its revision of ideas in the face of evidence. Science and scientists are committed to this ideal, and what's more, keep on doing it. Science calls for us to conform our theories to the information, and not the other way around. This honesty and brutal determination to stick to reality is probably its greatest achievement.

It is not surprising that science has been seen, throughout the twentieth century, as the ideal model of intellectual pursuit. By the 1960s, it seemed that all academic disciplines were clamouring to be known as a science—history, economics, linguistics. To be considered a science was to make a sociological appeal for authority. Politicians wishing to support their policies, lobby groups with various social or environmental aims, business interests, social engineers; all appealed to science to back their claims. It was a powerful ploy; science *did* hold social authority, and with good reason.

Even so, the limitations of science are rarely discussed and often unappreciated by the very scientists who practise it. Philosophically, the limitations should always have been recognized (and originally were explicit)—science studies the workings of the material world, and so cannot make pronouncements one way or the other on God, metaphysics, ethics and so on; it certainly cannot declare them meaningless. These ideas have been discussed extensively elsewhere and I will not go into them here.[10] But more than that, science and its genuine claims for factual authority have been corrupted because of its usefulness in polemics of all sorts.

We are used to science being appealed to by every side in political debates. The vast business interests involved in energy production can find scientific research that discredits global warming while environmental groups cite studies that support the theory.[11] Science is used to prove any number of things about the effects of smoking tobacco, and despite all claims of honesty, there still seems to be a strange correlation between studies funded by the tobacco industry and pro-smoking results.[12] It is not surprising that, in the debate over genetically modified foods, it seems that scientific arguments are having little effect on the general public's mood.[13] People just don't trust scientific claims any more. The tendency of lobby groups, journalists and even funds-seeking scientists to take tentative scientific conclusions and turn them into headline-making definite pronouncements means that too many times, science has been seen to prove whatever anyone wants it to. The very power of science as an authority has led to its corruption in the public view.

Moreover, science and its consequent technology has brought us much that is distasteful; dirty rivers, industrial accidents, dangerous radiation. While time after time the advances of science have enabled us to fix some short-term problem (demand for energy, food, consumer goods), we have created a long-term problem along with it (poor air quality, erosion, pollution). In the public view, science too often represents faceless, heartless, corporate rationalism with no concern for ordinary people. It is interesting that in current popular culture, the romantic and intuitive side often battles against the rationalist. Consider *Star Wars*, in which Luke turns off his computerized targeting system, trusting his feelings and the Force; or *The X-Files*, where the intuitive Mulder was constantly found to be right in his irrational opposition to the scientific Scully.

But one area in which the real value of science has been totally distorted, and by the very apologists who claim to be defending science against its enemies, is the highly irrational use of science to battle religion. Atheist 'defenders' of science are very quick to grab scientific hypotheses to disprove God, and rarely (if ever) retract their statements if their hypothesis is found wanting. The war against religion is in the background of all popular science discussion. Try finding a book on evolutionary theory that does not at some point deride creationism, or spend an inordinate amount of time 'proving' that evolution is a fact, not a theory. Has any television show on the history of science ever mentioned Galileo without accusing the church of opposing science? The polemical use of science to discredit God and Christianity is so common it is hard to imagine popular science without it.[14]

Rejection of God

The rejection of God in science is all part of our culture's slow move away from Christianity as the dominant philosophy of Western civilization. The eighteenth century saw the move from Christianity, with its emphasis on the special revelation of God in the Bible, to deism, which denied special revelation in favour of general revelation. It was a move that many Christians thought they could live with, for there *is* general revelation; it is quite true that God, the creator, demonstrates something of himself in the world. But the shift made it that much easier to slide from deism out of Christianity altogether. Within Christianity, liberal theology did its part by rejecting the old, biblical roots of the religion, keeping only those doctrines consistent with human reason—or at least, consistent with the reason of whatever human happened to be writing.[15]

So the Western intellect gradually moved away from Christian thought. The problem was, it was assumed that we could keep Christian morality without revelation. Then it was thought that we could keep any workable morality without revelation. Reason and common sense alone would enable us to run an ethical, fair, just, compassionate society in which people's rights were respected and evil not allowed. It was thought that, without an external authority, human thought alone could create a liveable world. We were wrong.

✣

Cultural shifts take a long time, and they are rarely pursued rationally. People may embrace new ideas, but will keep their old assumptions. The framers of the constitution of the United States may not have been explicitly Christian—their language is more deistic than Christian—but intentionally or not, they still believed in a Christian form of deism. They regarded it as self-evident that all men are *created* equal. They had moved far enough away from specifically Christian ideas to put their trust in a more generic God rather than Jesus Christ; but it was still 'God', not 'the gods'. It was certainly not the Force (or an eighteenth-century counterpart). The Christian framework survived long after its particular tenets had been denied. Even now, in this rationalistic and multicultural age, we have debates about the separation of church and state—not the separation of temple and state, or mosque and state. The Christian idea still frames our discussion.

Nonetheless, it can't last forever. Christianity has been overtly rejected so often, its specific claims denied and its basis criticized, that in general it is no longer a publicly accepted philosophy. Even its lingering assumptions about the value of human life and concepts of virtue are being worn away. Over time, if the basis of Christianity is denied often enough, such assumptions won't hold water. This is despite the fact that the majority of the population probably still holds to the basically Christian world view —but those who control *public* discussion, in the media, books, film, drama, art, television and so on, have rejected Christianity in favour of an atheistic or agnostic alternative.

But the alternative creates a monster.

A doomed project

Once society is set up on atheistic, rationalistic and scientific grounds, it must fail. It is not just that ours happened to fail, or that with different leaders or states it might not have failed; an atheistic society will, inevitably, fail. There are several reasons.

We are not machines

The world, and people in particular, simply do not operate on the basis of measurable, reductionist explanations. It is a wrong assumption that the methodology of examining the inanimate can be applied to the animate (let alone the human). To some extent, we have recognized the danger inherent in studying animate beings (such as animals) in the same way as we study the inanimate. We now reject techniques such as vivisection, cutting up live animals as if they had no more feeling than lumps of rock. But we still have some way to go in recognizing that we make the same mistake in thinking that humans can be studied, and understood properly, as animals. When researchers evaluate humans, they have a subject that can look back, and evaluate the researcher. It is not surprising that when using such methods the level of certainty decreases as the subjects of investigation move from animals, to humans, and to groups of humans. And yet we still think we can use reductionistic scientific method to understand, or dismiss, something greater than humans—such as God.

Utilitarianism does not work

The scientific society was bound to fail because it brings metaethical assumptions back in, even to deny metaethics. For instance, to say that humans are only animals, or that animals have no rights, or that they do have rights, is to make ethical statements. As soon as animals or humans are valued differently from atoms, ethical values have been introduced. What's more, such ethics are arational—where do they come from? What is the (scientific) basis for such a judgement?

Utilitarianism seems to be an easy answer because it sounds good. Its basis for ethics is quite simple: the good thing to do is that which creates happiness for the greatest number of people. Whether the issue is pornography, censorship, drugs, shooting-rooms, experiments on embryos, marriage or sex, utilitarianism says we do not need to turn to religious scruples to find the right answer; we decide on the basis of what works best. What approach actually makes human lives happiest?

At face value, utilitarian ethics are hard to argue against. Of course we want to make people's lives better. Any society that deliberately works against the wellbeing of its citizens would appear monstrous. But we do not need to scratch very deep to find some glaring weaknesses with utilitarianism as a theory. For one, just what is happiness? Is it really the highest good for people? How many people need to be happy to have a success? What if, for a significant number of people, torture makes them happy? How unhappy do the minority have to be before the happiness of the majority is questioned?

There have been many discussions of utilitarian ethics on various levels; I do not intend to cover all the theory here. Rather, I would like to point out a few strictly practical problems with utilitarian ethics.[16] The appeal of utilitarianism is largely in its practicality; we don't have to work out on some grand scale what is right and wrong, just what works best for our society. But it is precisely at that point that utilitarian ethics fail.

If utilitarianism were to work properly, we would have to be free to experiment on people and on society to determine what works best, what brings about the best results. But this we cannot do, for societies are not the sort of things you can experiment on. I am not referring at this point to ethical concerns about exploiting people, or informed consent and so on—although they are a strong enough barrier. No, there are very practical problems that prevent a scientific approach to the social good, or the application of utilitarian ethics.

1. We cannot have a control group when running tests on society. We cannot test freedom from censorship, or a change in sexual morality, on just one isolated part of society, keeping the rest of it pure. Of course, one part of society could be locked up—but again, apart from ethical concerns, this will not work, for then the society being studied would have been been radically changed. Society is not like agriculture or petri dishes, where one area can be sown with one organism and another with another, and results compared. Society may be sown with a new idea or practice, but not under

scientifically controlled conditions.

2. Related to the above problem, and even more important, is that society can't go back once the experiment is over. An experimental field can be re-ploughed, and taken back to what it was. A petri dish can be thrown out once it has been used, and a new one prepared. That can't be done with society. Once we've tried a social experiment, we're stuck with the results it has produced, no matter how disastrous.

3. In any case, the idea that we *do* try out new ideas as social experiments is an illusion—for even when they don't work, we do nothing to stop them. We don't have a scientific attitude to society; neither do our legislators, or social engineers, or media commentators. Having discarded theological considerations in determining our behaviour, we now simply do what we like, *regardless of whether it works or not*. Consider the wholesale abandonment of life-long commitment in marriage, as one example. Study after study has shown that cohabitation as trial marriage doesn't work.[17] Marriages after cohabitation are far more likely to break down than marriages conducted the traditional way. Cohabitation itself is demonstrably bad for people, on the whole; both men and women suffer more stress, less satisfaction, their children do worse at school and everyone's health suffers compared to traditional marriages. But we are making no effort to stop or discourage the practice. Neither social education, nor peer pressure, nor public example, nor tax breaks, nor any other way of influencing public behaviour—in fact, all the ways that

were used to make cohabitation acceptable in the first place—are being used to try to stop this now demonstrably harmful practice.

The scientific society—the society that is meant to be run by rational, trial and error principles, not by abstract religious morality—has failed. The society that was meant to adopt ethics based on the outcome of behaviours and whether they helped or harmed people—that society has never emerged. It was always bound to fail, for the idea is unworkable. Without divine foreknowledge, we cannot know in advance what behaviour will hurt or harm society—and even when we find out, we don't care. The scientific experiment has been profoundly irrational, and has not led to a better society. All it has done is unhinged the philosophical basis for a society that did work, whether we liked it or not—the theological one.

✠

One dubious, but undeniable effect of the social experiment that was the scientific society is that it has been quite deliberately, and quite irrationally, anti-God. This has always been part of the agenda in creating a scientific, secularist society. It is an unnecessary bias, forced on science by prejudice, but it is definitely there. Evolutionists such as the late Stephen Jay Gould and Richard Dawkins may have been at loggerheads for years over their competing theories, but they stood shoulder to shoulder against any idea of creation. Science has for the past two centuries been consistently sidetracked by the anti-Christian bias of certain prominent scientists. Sometimes, after the event, it emerges that the opposition to Christianity had its root in private, personal immorality—such as the example of Margaret Mead, whose 'scientific' data supporting an anti-Christian view was found to be largely a matter of fraud and mistake.[18]

It is, ultimately, a self-defeating attitude, for it is belief in God—the Christian, Protestant God in particular—that gave birth to experimental science, the collective effort to discover the working of an understandable and rational universe, as an activity worthy of human endeavour.[19] The universe in Protestant Christianity is something we can study, in the expectation of discovering its workings. Moreover, if we want to discover the workings of the universe, we must observe it and experiment upon it, for we cannot work out from abstract first principles how a freely creative God *must* have done things.

So unlike medieval rationalism, that sought to unravel the necessary world from given first principles, and unlike Buddhism or Hinduism which see the material world as a chaotic prison to be escaped from, it was Protestant Christianity which saw the world as God's good and orderly creation, and thus gave the Western world science.

The shape of failure

We have tried the experiment of constructing a rational, science-based society. We have created the secularist society dreamed of by nineteenth-century freethinkers, run by scientists as the greatest intellectual authority, as Thomas Huxley wanted. We have a society based on utilitarian ethics, as Bertrand Russell advocated. We have dispensed with the Christian rationale for morality, as George Eliot wished. And so we have created a just, sane society based on truth and reason, in which all humans are considered equal and treated well in a healthy, happy society. We wish.

What we have actually created is a crazy society of fractured relationships and broken people, with little hope that there is any truth or that anyone knows it.

Postmodernism

One thing we have created is postmodernism—which is only the logical extension of a philosophy based on atheism. Postmodernism points out that if there is no external reference point against which to judge morality, rationality, meaning and truth, then we ourselves—each one of us—are the ultimate arbiters of what is true for us. If there is no ultimate right or wrong, then it comes down to my judgement as to whether my actions are right or wrong. I only have my own opinion as to what is truth or falsity, or beauty or ugliness, or anything else. What else can I base it on? Your judgement? The collective judgement? Why should it be any better than mine?[20]

Postmodernism is the implosion of rationalism, and it was inevitable once people really started thinking about the basis for their secularist beliefs. Rationalism caved in on itself—for why value rationalism above, say, intuition? Romanticism wins—after all, it feels so much nicer. Meaning becomes flexible—after all, the meaning that *I* perceive is the only one available to me. What *you* meant is a different thing entirely, and I don't have access to that. The result can seem ridiculous, when we spend more time reading between the lines than reading them, but why should we not if we are the only arbiters of the meaning of a text? To the horror of scientists, even scientific 'truth' is now questioned, with its inbuilt assumptions about the possibility of objective observation and conclusions.[21]

Postmodernism contains a profound truth, one which we can't easily evade. Modernism *was* inadequate. We cannot build an edifice of truth upon reason alone, for who is to say we can trust our reason? Ourselves? Postmodernism is right—there is no foundation, no centre; if we ourselves are the only bastions of truth, then there are as many truths as there are people.

However postmodernism is only right as an analysis of the universe without God. But in this universe, postmodernists come across a fundamental problem: for there *is* truth; there is meaning, and we can communicate it—indeed we do so every day. Postmodernism is right in criticizing moderns for thinking that this daily practice of believing in truth, justice, communication, meaning and reality makes any sense without an external basis—without God. If we want to hold only these things—and we must, for we know they are real, and we cannot live without them—then we must give up on the foolishness of atheistic secularism. It renders us, ultimately, unable even to talk about the things that really matter. We cannot have any real ethical discussion on the basis of secularist philosophy, for there is no ultimate starting point on which we agree. When is a baby a baby and not just a foetus? How do we tell? Why do we care? The most basic questions about who we are as humans must remain unanswered. If all we have are ourselves—accidentally intelligent animals in a meaningless universe—the answers to these questions are just too unpalatable. They make us into nothing.

What is more, if there is nothing more to the universe than ourselves and our opinions, then evil is only a matter of opinion. But we know that some things *are* evil. The tyranny of Stalin, Pol Pot, Mao—all, by the way, utilitarians trying to create the secularist scientific society—were evil. The barbarity of Idi Amin was evil. Paedophilia, pack rape, kidnapping and drug pushing are evil. But we cannot with any consistency call these evils 'evil' when there is no absolute, but only personal values. If we only have ourselves as the absolute arbiters of everything, then we only have individual opinions and no basis on which to judge them.

We have failed to run a just society on a utilitarian basis. We deny the existence of virtues; we insist that there are only 'good outcomes', and we seem incapable of producing those. Questions of life and death have no way of being decided, because the outcomes are things we don't and can't know. And so our society falls back to the only basis for value it is able to maintain in this material world, the only absolute way of determining what is good and bad, worthy or unworthy—economics.

Economics

The utilitarian failure has left us with the economic society. The only strategy governments seem to have in the Western world is economic; their goal is to expand the nation's economy. It's fairly simple to see why this is the overriding strategy, for what else is there? A president who tries to justify a war on the basis of moral right causes untold division, and not only because we can't agree what moral right is; he's also just plain not believed. "Don't tell me about sweat, blood, tears and toil; it's all about the price of oil", sings Billy Bragg.[22] Governments simply are not in the business of moral right and wrong any more; they can't be, in a world when such discussions simply make no sense. But money—that's something we can agree on. Better still, we can put a number to it, so we can *know* when we're succeeding. More money is good, less is bad—that's what we have been reduced to.[23]

It's an illusion, of course, not least because more money does not actually make us happier.[24] But it's still something to cling to. It gives a nice, clear basis on which to make decisions. As economic beings, we don't have to worry about the impossible question of good and bad, just profit and loss. It's definite. We can understand the answers, and we enjoy the perks of winning the game.

The result is that the only things with value are the things that make money. Work is only valuable and worthwhile if it makes money. Volunteerism has been eroded as a result—we see this in the wholesale withdrawal of volunteers from charities, Girl Guides and Boy Scouts, political parties, community activities and so on. The idea that a person might give his or her life to voluntary work simply because it's a good thing to do, because of the non-economic good it does to others—that just doesn't work any more.

In particular, the volunteer work of a mother with her family is downgraded. Looking after someone else's family can, possibly, be an exception—if the child carer is qualified and, of course, paid to do so. That's a fulfilling career. But a mother who gives up paid work to look after her own children, for no better reason than that she thinks it's good for them—she's looked down upon for not working. She's not even in the running for those considered 'successful'. For that, she has to be earning money.

The trend towards viewing money as the only effective value is something obvious and lamentable in society. The examples are numerous: the mutual societies which floated as companies because the idea of simply existing to help people, not to make money, wasn't valid any more; the governments that are considered successful only when the country experiences economic growth; the campaigns by environmentalists to have 'environmental cost' put on the balance sheet—and the problems of working out how to do so, because it's not the kind of value that goes by numbers. Various social theorists have tried to promote 'social capital' as a real concept—the intangible value of things like relationships, family ties and the strength they provide people—but we really don't know what to do with these concepts.[25] We can't give them numbers, they don't fit well into graphs and statistics, and they don't fit into our pockets at the end of the day. So how can they be real?

We resent this development in society, because we know that people and families and trust and so on *do* have value, quite independently of the money they have or earn; but we don't know how to measure or recognize or even really speak about such value. The Australian Senate had to put a financial cost on marriage breakdown before it could be understood as a truly bad thing.[26]

Perhaps the perfect example of the economic basis of our values is the inability of our governments to deal with the problem of gambling. Gambling is a terrible industry that ruins people, families and communities. But *it makes money*—in particular, it makes a lot of money for the government. In the only scale that counts, gambling is a winner. So here we have something overwhelmingly recognized as harmful—even by our government representatives themselves—but there is nothing they can or will do about it.

The values provided by economics are empty ones. They only thing we can agree on as a 'good'—making money—is one not really worth having. All the other things—the values we need, involving people and how to treat them, of life, love and liberty and how best to protect them, the values of community and working together and helping each other—all the things that really matter—we can't make sense of any more. Society has gone for too long without any coherent teaching or framework on which to ground them. We are groping blindly for something to hang values on. The exodus of children from public schools to a large extent reflects this. Their parents are voting with their children's feet—voting against the so-called 'value free' secularist education the public schools provide, which is not so much free of values as free of any coherent framework in which to have them.

We do talk about other values, of course, and use them to promote some things as good and others as bad. We don't put absolutely everything in money terms; that is just the dominant value. But the other 'values' we hold turn out to be just as empty, because they mean whatever we want—or rather, whatever the strongest lobby group wants. We turn to those now.

Tolerance and tyranny

While our only real and quantifiable values are economic, we still talk of certain intangibles as moral standards. They can be summarized by the catch-cry 'tolerance'. In itself, tolerance is a well-defined concept with a worthy history. In the absence of a coherent ethical framework, however, it is easily perverted. The tolerant society has become a shouting match between lobby groups, with the loudest voices winning.

Tolerance is a good thing to cultivate, but it only makes sense in the context of an agreed moral framework. For what is it, precisely, that we are called upon to tolerate? What are the boundaries of tolerance? When are we allowed to become intolerant?[27]

The problem is revealed in tolerance's opposite. As the flip-side of our pretend value, we have a pretend condemnation: 'un-Australian'. It is a totally vacuous condemnation in a tolerant society, but it is still the ultimate putdown. But if multiculturalism, the practical clothing of tolerance, is true, then there is no such thing as 'Australian' to start with. If every culture in our country is to be accepted as valid, then they are all as Australian as each other. If we accept *all* cultures as having a right to exist, if this is how Australia is made up, then any one of them is Australian, and no member of any culture can be 'un-Australian'. But of course, even in our world of pretend values, people don't *really* believe all cultures have a right to exist. People want to exclude fascists or communists or racists or paedophiles or fundamentalists. From time to time, all of us in different ways want to condemn someone. We want to exclude certain cultures that we don't want. But when no one culture is allowed to be seen as bad, we are driven to the meaningless criticism, 'un-Australian'.

But what is Australian? And who decides? Is a billionaire un-Australian for trying to avoid paying taxes? In that case, any Australian is un-Australian. Are cricket players who sledge each other un-Australian? They are more likely to be representative of Australians, sadly, if they do. Just who is un-Australian? We don't know, because we're supposed to be tolerant of everyone. But we don't want to be tolerant of all; and the more that certain lobby groups control our ideas, the less tolerant we all become. Tolerance sounds good; but its outworking is that the strongest and sneakiest win. The ones who know best how to manipulate public opinion.

To have tolerance as our primary ethic is a pretence, and a dangerous one. It means there is no universal basis for excluding anyone any more, and so any group smart enough can potentially grab power—and so reverse any 'tolerance' they don't happen to like. Interest groups are doing it to us all the time; affecting public opinion not on the basis of evidence, or good arguments, or reason, but simply because to oppose them is not 'tolerant'. And so we end up with a mishmash of opinions that make little sense, and that can be utterly intolerant.

Let us draw together the threads. We have seen in general terms that the problems of Western society can be related to an underlying philosophical loss of direction. We have been travelling down this path for a long time, and we are now suffering the consequences. At this point, it is natural that I would turn to the Bible for a solution.

Doesn't the Bible have a solution?

The Bible does indeed have a solution, which most people would be aware of, but that is not the main point I wish to make. What many would not be aware of is that the Bible said this would happen. The Bible has always accurately diagnosed humans and how they are likely to behave. In particular, the Bible has said for thousands of years that when people turn away from God, they do not become independent, free-thinking atheists; instead, it predicts, they will become confused, intolerant, close-minded people who treat each other badly.

The New Testament, for instance, speaks of people, who "although they knew God, did not honour him as God or give thanks to him" (Rom 1:21, ESV). The intellectual effect of this refusal to accept the reality of God is inevitable: "they became futile in their thinking, and their foolish hearts were darkened. Claiming to be wise, they became fools" (Rom 1:21-22, ESV). What is even more telling is what the Bible predicts about the behaviour that will follow:

> Therefore God gave them up in the lusts of their hearts to impurity, to the dishonouring of their bodies among themselves, because they exchanged the truth about God for a lie and worshipped and served the creature rather than the Creator ... And since they did not see fit to acknowledge God, God gave them up to a debased mind to do what ought not to be done. They were filled with all manner of unrighteousness, evil, covetousness, malice. They are full of envy, murder, strife, deceit, maliciousness. They are gossips, slanderers, haters of God, insolent, haughty, boastful, inventors of evil, disobedient to parents, foolish, faithless, heartless, ruthless.[28]

So Christians are not surprised. In fact, while we can say our social experiment with atheism has been an horrific failure, incidentally it has been a very successful test of the truth of the Bible. What the Bible predicted has happened. As people turn from God, they become materialists and hedonists, to their own hurt. To the hurt of all of us.

The Bible also gives the solution, but until we start to see the problem, our society can't begin to be healed. Until we recognize that the basis of our problem lies in our turning away from God, we probably will not listen to the Bible or even suspect that it has anything worthwhile to say. Nonetheless, the answer is there, and is freely available.

ENDNOTES

1   National Drug Strategy, *Alcohol in Australia: Issues and Strategies*, July 2001, p. 19.
2   National Drug Strategy, *ibid.*, pp. 7-8.
3   Apart from obvious personal/anecdotal evidence, some more technical studies demonstrate this. For recent studies on the importance of marriage and children, see Philip Hughes and Alan Black, 'Social capital and family life', paper presented to the 8th AIFS conference, February 2003; Michael Shields and Mark Wooden, 'Marriage, children and subjective well-being', paper presented to the Australian Institute of Family Studies Conference, Melbourne, February 2003; and Jody Hughes and Wendy Stone, 'Family change and community life: exploring the links', Australian Institute of Family Studies, Research Paper no. 32, April 2003. There are a multitude of such studies available.
4   Data from *To Have and to Hold: a report of the inquiry into aspects of family services,* House of Representatives Standing Committee on Legal and Constitutional Affairs, Canberra, 1998, pp. 6-12.

5 'The Invisible Disease: Depression', National Institute of Mental Health, http://www.nimh.nih.gov/publicat/invisible.cfm; See also 'The World Today', ABC News Online, http://www.abc.net.au/worldtoday/s66594.htm.

6 See Ben Cooper, 'After the wind: the pursuit of happiness through economic progress', *kategoria*, 1999, 13, pp. 9-24.

7 As John Ralston Saul has pointed out, it made economic sense in the 70s to expand the arms trade—one of the problems with basing decisions upon economics. See my review of Saul's books in this collection of essays.

8 See Warren Sylvester Smith, *The London Heretics 1870-1914*, Constable, London, 1967, especially pp. 27-83. The coining of 'secularism' is similar to Thomas Henry Huxley's coining of the word 'agnostic' as a nicer word than 'atheist' and thus helpful for his anti-Christian agenda. Adrian Desmond, *Huxley: Evolution's High Priest*, Michael Joseph, London, 1997, p. 249.

9 See Adrian Desmond, *ibid.*, vols I and II; also Kirsten Birkett, *Unnatural Enemies*, Matthias Media, Sydney, 1998 for a summary of this process. David Starling, in 'Thomas Huxley and the 'warfare' between science and religion: mythology, politics and ideology', *kategoria*, 1996, 3, pp. 33-50 discusses a particular and crucial battle in the battle for scientific supremacy.

10 See Birkett, *Unnatural Enemies, op. cit.* for an introduction to this discussion.

11 As seen in the surprising furor caused by Bjorn Lomborg's *The Skeptical Environmentalist: Measuring the Real State of the World*, Cambridge University Press, Cambridge, 1998. Readers of *New Scientist* magazine will be familiar with the political manoeuvres on this issue; for an index of many articles, see the page on climate change, http://www.newscientist.com/hottopics/climate/.

12 See, for instance, 'Controversy over passive smoking danger', *New Scientist*, 16th May 2003, available on the New Scientist website http://www.newscientist.com/news/news.jsp?id=ns999 93737, along with links to similar articles.

13 Articles such as 'GM food safety fear "based on distortion"', *New Scientist* 25th June 2003, http://www.newscientist.com/news/news.jsp?id=ns99993874 or 'GM food risk to humans "very low"', *New Scientist* 21st July 2003, http://www.newscientist.com/

news/print.jsp?id=ns99993959.

14 For a discussion of the ubiquity of religious discussion in popular science, see Kirsten Birkett, *The Essence of Darwinism*, Matthias Media, Sydney, 2001, especially Part 3.

15 To trace this kind of shift in Western thought, see books such as R. C. Beiser, *The Sovereignty of Reason: The Defense of Rationality in the Early English Enlightenment*, Princeton University Press, Princeton, 1996; and W. C. Placher, *The Domestication of Transcendence: How Modern Thinking about God went Wrong*, Westminster John Knox Press, Louisville, 1996. Danielle Scarratt reviews both of these books in 'How strong is your faith in reason?', *kategoria*, 2001, 23, pp. 65-87.

16 The classic text on utilitarian ethics is, of course, John Stuart Mill's *Utilitarianism*, available in several modern reprints. An excellent outline of utilitarian ethics with arguments for and against is J. J. C. Smart and Bernard Williams, *Utilitarianism: For and Against*, Cambridge University Press, Cambridge, 1973.

17 Some recent studies are Michael Shields and Mark Wooden, 'Marriage, children and subjective well-being', *op. cit*; and David de Vaus, Lixia Qu and Ruth Weston, 'Does premarital cohabitation affect the chances of marriage lasting?', paper presented at the eighth Australian Institute of Family Studies Conference, Melbourne, February 2003, available on the Australian Institute of Family Studies website, http://www.aifs.gov.au/institute/afrc8/papers.html#d. There are many more studies reported in *To Have and to Hold, op. cit*.

18 See my essay in this volume on Mead; for some other interesting stories, see Paul Johnson, *Intellectuals*, Harper and Row, New York, 1988.

19 See Colin A. Russell, *Cross-currents: Interactions between Science and Faith*, IVP, Leicester, 1985, especially chapter 4; Donald M. McKay, *The Clockwork Image: A Christian Perspective on Science*, IVP, London, 1974; Gary B. Deason, 'Reformation theology and the mechanistic conception of nature', in David C. Lindberg and Ronald L. Numbers (eds), *God and Nature: Historical Essays on the Encounter between Christianity and Science*, University of California Press, Berkeley, 1986, pp. 167-191.

20 For a secular(ist) introduction to postmodernism, see

David Harvey, *The Condition of Postmodernity*, Blackwell, Oxford, 1990; a Christian discussion is Gene Edward Veith, *Postmodern Times*, Crossway Books, Wheaton, 1994.

21 See the horrified responses encapsulated within books such as Paul R. Gross and Norman Levitt, *Higher Superstition: The Academic Left and its Quarrels with Science*, Johns Hopkins University Press, Baltimore, 1994.

22 Billy Bragg, 'The price of oil', on *Sounds of dissent: the politics of music,* produced by New Internationalist, 2003.

23 For an excellent discussion of this, see Peter Kaldor, 'The economic point of view', *kategoria*, 2000, 17, pp. 11-24.

24 Many commentators, even economists, are beginning to recognize this. Ross Gittins, an economist who writes regularly for *The Sydney Morning Herald*, has published a number of articles along these lines. See for instance 'More delivers us much less', 17/9/03.

25 If you are interested in the idea of social capital, see papers from the Australian Institute of Family Studies website, such as Wendy Stone, 'Measuring social capital', Research Paper no. 24, Australian Institute of Family Studies, February 2001, http://www.aifs.org.au/institute/pubs/stone.html; or Ian Winter 'Towards a theorised understanding of family life and social capital', Working Paper no. 21, Australian Institute of Family Studies, April 2000, http://www.aifs.org.au/institute/pubs/winter4.html.

26 *To Have and to Hold, op. cit.*, p. xiv.

27 See Phil Miles, 'Of truth, tolerance and tyranny', *kategoria*, 2001, 22, pp. 7-27 and 23, pp. 5-26.

28 Romans 1:24-31, ESV.

2.
Coming of age in controversy
Margaret Mead, Derek Freeman and intellectual leadership

SYDNEY HAS ENJOYED the release of many plays by Australia's premier playwright, David Williamson. One of the most popular was *Heretic*. It is a play about ideas: the anthropological controversy between Margaret Mead and Derek Freeman. It was itself a controversial play, with disagreements between the playwright and the director providing much newsprint. Because of Williamson's views about intellectual life, which he has openly discussed, it has also brought to public attention issues of academic integrity and intellectual leadership.

The play has transformed an academic debate into public entertainment. In fact, the debate was already fairly public. Derek Freeman in 1983 launched a book not just into academic halls, but into the general media, especially in America. The publicity surrounding the launch basically claimed that the book would completely destroy Margaret Mead's credibility. Freeman did not just criticise Mead's theory; he insisted that her very research was so poor that her evidence was virtually non-existent. It made marvellous media conflict, for Mead had been tremendously influential for years, and members of the public could legitimately consider themselves stakeholders in the debate. Nevertheless, although the media might have loved Freeman, the anthropological community rejected him, and defended its heroine, Mead. It appears, in the eyes of several commentators at least, that more was at stake than just the evidence each of them cited.

This is not the place to analyse in detail the merits of the Mead-Freeman debate.[1] It is difficult to say who 'won', though Williamson's play came out fairly firmly in favour of Freeman. In the meantime, however, the play and Williamson's comments about intellectual life let us throw a few ideas into the melting pot about intellectual leadership.

Mead and Freeman: the play and real life

David Williamson's plays have grown in popularity and significance in Australia, and he is usually regarded as Australia's leading playwright. He has remained on the cutting edge of the community's thinking and mood-shifts, and presented complex ideas in a popularly acceptable form. *Heretic,* which opened in early 1996 at the Sydney Opera House, is a well researched and entertaining attempt to present a controversy that has been at work in anthropological circles many years now.

Derek Freeman, the emeritus professor of anthropology at the Australian National University, is the heretic of Williamson's play. It is an appropriate title, for in one sense Freeman is formally a heretic; in Chicago in November 1983, the American Anthropological Association passed a motion denouncing his work as "unscientific". Williamson also puts Freeman in the broader context as one who stood out against the anthropologist's credo of cultural relativism. Derek Freeman took sides on the nature/nurture debate and argued for nature, against the overwhelming tide of anthropological opinion which was in favour of nurture.

Margaret Mead was one of the champions of the nurture argument. The research of Margaret Mead in Samoa in the 1920s is presented in the play as being a critical demonstration of the teachings of Margaret Mead's mentor, Franz Boas. Boas, who wrote the forward in Margaret Mead's book, *Coming of Age in Samoa*,[2] argued for cultural relativism rather than the absolutes of nature. In particular, Boas and Mead were challenging the view that the 'storm and stress' of adolescent development is an inevitable part of growing up—simply part of human 'nature'. By examining a society largely unaffected by our Western culture and nurturing—one which, in Mead's view, showed no signs of the stress of adolescent development—Mead sought to demonstrate that adolescent turmoil is not a function of our nature, but our nurture. In Boas' forward we read:

> In our own civilisation the individual is beset with difficulties which we are likely to ascribe to fundamental human traits. When we speak about the difficulties of childhood and of adolescence, we are thinking of them as unavoidable periods of adjustment through which everyone has to pass. The whole psycho-analytic approach is largely based on this supposition.

> The anthropologist doubts the correctness of these views, but up to this time hardly anyone has taken the pains to identify himself sufficiently with a primitive population to obtain an insight into these problems. We feel, therefore, grateful to Miss Mead for having undertaken to identify herself so completely with Samoan youth that she gives us a lucid and clear picture of the joys and difficulties encountered by the young individual in a culture so entirely different from our own. The results of her painstaking investigation confirm the suspicion long held by anthropologists, that much of what we ascribe to human nature is no more than a reaction to the restraints put upon us by our civilisation.[3]

This book became the anthropological best seller of the century. In it Mead claimed to have found such differences in culture between Samoa and the West that it would explain fundamental differences in adolescent experience. Nature, she hoped to have demonstrated, is not the determinant of our behaviour; we are products of cultural nurturing.

Derek Freeman, on the other hand, did not accept that nurture is so overwhelmingly important. In his view, Mead's theory was the end result of philosophical presuppositions that go back to the British philosopher John Locke. It is a commitment to the idea that humans are born with minds that are *tabula rasa*; that is, "... empty tablets capable of receiving all sorts of imprints but having none stamped on them by nature".[4] In other words,

Freeman considered that social anthropologists were working not out of evolutionary scientific understanding, but out of a philosophical commitment to this egalitarian ideology, in seeking to establish the importance of nurture over nature. Their conclusions did not arise from observational data; rather, anthropologists were confirmed in their presuppositions by Mead's Samoan study.

Freeman was not totally opposed to the concept of nurture as determinative. He acknowledged that nurture and culture both have some part to play in governing the direction of human behaviour. He wanted, however, to argue for the existence of natural determinants of behaviour. Freeman insisted upon an interactionist model of human behaviour, with nature and nurture affecting each other as humans make choices: "Heredity and environment interact and modify behaviour at every stage of development".[5] We are not empty tablets as John Locke expected, and Mead's "extreme environmentalist conclusions of 1928 cannot conceivably be correct".[6] For Derek Freeman,

> the making of choices is ... one of the crucially significant biologically-given capacities of members of the human species, and so becomes a quite fundamental element in any interactionist paradigm.[7]

Most of Derek Freeman's adult life is portrayed in David Williamson's play as directed against the predominant 'nurture' paradigm of his professional colleagues. The point of conflict was his study of Samoa and controversy with Margaret Mead. Hers was the flagship of anthropological cultural relativism. Hers was the work that he studied and from his own experience found inadequate. While he challenged her in writing and in person it wasn't until after her death in 1983 that he produced his major work on the subject.[8] Here he exposed the empirical inadequacies of Mead's work in Samoa. Here also the controversy came down upon his head, for while the media and many scholars came to accept his critique, if not demolition, of Margaret Mead's studies, the anthropological community of North America gathered in her defence and attacked Derek Freeman critically and personally.

The controversy continued through the 1980s with one significant point of advance in 1987. Fa'apua'a Fa'amu, the Samoan woman on whose testimony Mead had based most of her conclusions about Samoan culture, came forward in 1987 and testified that, as a game, she and a friend tricked Mead back in 1925 and 1926. The two girls were apparently telling Mead lies that fitted in with the kinds of questions she was asking.[9]

While to Freeman and many in the world this testimony was the clinching piece of evidence, the debate has continued to this day, with people casting doubts even on the evidence of Fa'apua'a Fa'amu.[10] However, Williamson's play reaches its climax with the testimony of Fa'apua'a Fa'amu and accepts that Freeman got it right.

✣

For a play to be written on such an abstract debate requires a focus on the personalities and conflict between them. Even though Mead and Freeman rarely met, and Mead hardly operated in the context of conflict with Freeman, Williamson still manages to present the play as a story about people. Mead is presented as more than a research scientist writing reports; she is a personality, a networker, a media persona, an advocate of ideas for change within American society based on her researches in primitive cultures. Freeman is a man who studies and struggles, with a well-publicized breakdown in mid-life which gives rise to questions as to why he wanted to take on the academic establishment. Williamson as playwright works out the controversy between these two personalities, particularly in relationship to their lifestyle, contrasting Mead's high profile, multiple marriages and sexual promiscuity, with Freeman's struggling, monogamous relationship.

This was not just artistic license, a playwright creating personal tension in order to convey abstract ideas in concrete forms. The Mead-Freeman controversy indeed was one that went beyond ideas into the very people involved in them. Margaret Mead was a 'larger than life' personality, who purposely wrote up her research for popular reception and openly entered into public debate. Freeman's controversy with her *did* point to the inadequacies of Mead the person, and not just of the research of Samoa. He wrote in a forceful, and what many found abrasive, style. Consequently, in the book by James E. Côté which analyses the debate, the personalities of the two combatants form a key part of the discussion and evaluation of their controversy.

The Sydney production of this play was given a further controversial edge by a public falling out between the director and the playwright. The director introduced elements into the production which displayed Margaret Mead as Marilyn Monroe, introduced 1960s music and dance in which she was seen to be 'the mother of us all', and presented Fa'apua'a Fa'amu in a grotesque, inhuman and unreal puppet head. Williamson objected strongly to these elements, to the show which trivialised his work, even misrepresenting it.[11]

It can only be a subjective evaluation, but on the evening on which I attended the play it seemed to me that both playwright and director were correct. The audience came to life at the very elements that the director had introduced to the play. It lifted the performance out of a serious and intellectual debate into a lively and commercially exciting presentation. However, it did seriously undermine the point of the play. The audience was not really left open to listen to the weight of the exposition of Freeman's critique of Mead's gospel of sexual liberation. Instead of history and data demonstrating Freeman's thesis in the testimony of a real historical person, strange, humorous stagecraft gave the final verdict. The curtain call was a joyous tribute to 60s sexual liberation. Without the director's trappings, the evening's experience would have been a more serious and powerful presentation of world views, but would no doubt have been far less entertaining. That in itself shows how much the members of the audience were the children of the Margaret Mead generation and philosophy; how influential Mead's views were and continue to be.

Mead, Freeman and intellectual leadership

The play was enjoyable, its plot tensions interesting. As Williamson has pointed out, however, the issue is more than just a dramatic controversy between public characters. "Derek's life has been the battle to establish the primacy of truth", Williamson commented at one point.[12] This play and its presentation expresses a certain disquiet that is beginning to be felt about the intellectual leadership given to our societies by the academic community. Leadership *is* provided by the academic community. Despite the indulgent portrayal of the ivory-tower professor, who is divorced from the 'real' world, the public pays a great deal of respect to academic opinion. "University tests prove" that anyone in a white coat can add considerable credibility to anything from washing powder to philosophy.

Within the academic world that people rely upon, however, things are often not so clear-cut. It is common to speak of scientific 'paradigms'. This word, popularised in the philosophy of science by Thomas Kuhn though it has proved extremely difficult to define,[13] is a useful short-hand for the general over-arching theory under which a community of scientists works. It is the general assumption behind most of the work of scientists in that community. As long as a paradigm is strong, minor discrepancies in specific experiments or case-studies can be explained away. For a paradigm to break down requires the scientists to be convinced of major errors in their work; and humans being the stubborn creatures they are, it happens sometimes that people hold onto cherished assumptions unreasonably. Freeman considers that his fight with Mead and her supporters is a matter of paradigms in conflict.

Margaret Mead was a—possibly the—leading anthropologist of her time. One anthropologist described her as "the preeminent leader of our field for decades".[14] The anthropological community, and indeed the academic community at large, relied upon her scholarship, and the paradigm she supported consequently became very strong. The academic backlash against Derek Freeman is a demonstration of the community's commitment to Mead's paradigm. For example, James Côté rejects the evidence of Fa'apua'a Fa'amu on the grounds of "mental acrobatics". He sees her as a Christian woman defending her own honour, who had not realised that her confessions about premarital sex that she had told an anthropologist privately would be broadcast across the world.[15] Also Freeman, in Côté's opinion, is motivated by his position as a *matai* rather than any intellectual pursuit of truth.[16]

What is more, Mead was a great advocate and populariser of her own ideas. She took her message directly to the public. She wrote her major book on the Samoan culture in such a fashion that the public at large could understand it. She encouraged the world to learn from her discoveries in Samoa and apply those lessons to other cultures. Hers was not the quiet intellectual debate advancing our understanding while recognising the severe limitations of our inquiries. She publicly preached and proclaimed cultural relativism with a subtext "anthropological tests prove ...".

It is easy to see around us in popular culture that this paradigm of the pre-eminence of nurture, and cultural relativism, still finds acceptance at popular levels. I noticed an incidental demonstration of its influence in the movie *Circle of Friends*, based on the novel by Maeve Binchy, which I watched on video around the same time I saw *Heretic*. The movie is set in Ireland in the late 1950s, when three young women attend their first year at university. During this year their Irish Catholic world view is to be shaken by their experiences and their classroom anthropological studies. Their handsome professor, a striking contrast to their hook-nosed and ugly Catholic priest, seeks to broaden their frame of reference by telling of the Trobrian Islanders in the works of Bronislaw Malinowski; a study parallel to Mead's work in Samoa. These anthropology lectures are not in the novel; they are inserted in the movie as a background to explain what is taking place as the women go through their first sexual encounters. The lecturer assures them that there is complete freedom of access between the sexes in the Trobrian Islands, from puberty to adolescence, and the people are "very happy and contented people". He speaks of the ways in which societies regulate the behaviour and conduct of their members by the use of the law, shame, guilt and fear. These 'vices' are amply illustrated, of course, in the portrayal of the Irish Catholic church. The film ends with the heroine writing a paper comparing the Irish Catholic mating rights with those of the Trobrian

Islanders, and implying that she has entered into a premarital sexual relationship with her boyfriend (again in contrast to the novel) with a voiceover ending the film, "Bless me, Father, for I have sinned".

Why was this anthropological background inserted into the movie? Perhaps it could be argued that the late 1950s experience of university life was in fact dominated by this kind of anthropological teaching to young men and women, who were struggling with their own sexual discoveries. Yet it can also be argued that its inclusion in the 1990s film—without comment, criticism or even implied challenge to these ideas—is an endeavour to perpetuate a particular ideological commitment.[17]

This movie also demonstrates what is easily observable in Western culture: that this particular scientific paradigm was not a neutral intellectual matter. It had direct consequences for society and the decisions of individuals. The academic world, which clearly provided leadership indicating that this paradigm was correct, should accept some responsibility for these consequences. Moreover, if Mead's actual work was wrong, as Derek Freeman has suggested, then the critical judgement of the scholarly consensus needs to be called into question. How and why have so many people of high academic standing been duped? This is a world-wide best-selling book, and possibly the most famous piece of anthropological research ever done. Why has it found such ready acceptance and been held up as a model for others to follow if, as Freeman suggests, it is so profoundly and fundamentally flawed?

The academic anthropological community has shown some prevarication—quick to defend itself and jump to Margaret Mead's aid, even while admitting privately that Mead was wrong. Professor Lowell Holmes, described by James Côté as the most qualified anthropologist to consult in this case,[18] said personally to Freeman, "I think it is quite true that Margaret finds pretty much what she wants to find ... While I was quite critical of many of her ideas and observations ... I was forced by my faculty adviser to soften my criticisms". He added "the only tragedy about Margaret is that she still refuses to accept the idea that she might have been wrong on her first field trip".[19] Yet Lowell Holmes wrote (at the time of Freeman's attack) in immediate defence of Margaret with titles such as, "The south sea squall; Derek Freeman's long nurtured, ill-natured attack on Margaret Mead".[20]

Perhaps an anthropological study on anthropologists is due. Under what cultural norms are they operating, whereby they think that moving majority motions in society association meetings is a method of establishing the truth or error, the scientific value or lack of scientific value, of the published work of fellow academics?[21] There are also questions about the wider political factors involved in decision making.[22] Why did the anthropological community believe Margaret Mead's Samoan story in the first place? Was it because it confirmed their paradigm of cultural relativism? Did it reinforce their 'nurture' view of the debate which gave legitimacy to their own discipline? Of course, this assumes that Mead was wrong. Many commentators have raised similar questions about Freeman and his motives and political agenda. Was he trying to score points by bringing down the tallest poppy in the land? Was he defending a traditional Samoan society because of his political status within that culture? Was his use of Freudian psychiatry to help him in his personal problems, a biasing factor against the anti-Freudian views of Boas and Mead?

✣

What is the social responsibility of academic leaders? Obviously there is a degree to which scientists cannot be blamed for holding inaccurate theories, if they are merely taking the most plausible explanation for the evidence available. Mead did far more than that, however. She set about popularizing her views and agitating for social change on the basis of them. It is this that has made the attack on her work such a public matter. This is no internal debate of scientists over competing theories; the general public who believed Mead has become involved. The anthropological community has been very annoyed at the way in which Freeman made his attack. They have complained that it was unacademic, and overly sensationalist, for Harvard University Press to play up the popular conflict and debate the issue in the newspapers before it had a chance to reach the anthropological journals.[23] Nevertheless, the popularizing Mead did herself could be taken to justify Freeman's public attack. Although academic protocol may have been breached, it was a larger population than just the academic community who were concerned in the truth or otherwise of her conclusions.

The main concern is that Freeman has thrown into severe doubt whether Mead's theories were based on good evidence at all. This is the crucial point. If Freeman's criticisms are correct, then the Mead-Freeman debate raises more than just questions of changing paradigms; it raises questions of academic integrity. No one can be right all the time, but the evidence on which an academic leader bases major theories should be sound, and the method for gathering that evidence beyond reproach.

It is worth pointing out that the Christian understanding has always asserted the inevitability of bias. As creatures in rebellion against our creator, we are not impartial beings, and especially we do not have moral autonomy. Belief in the value of investigation and the reality of the external world has always, in the Christian world view, been tempered by a knowledge of our immense capacity for self-deception. Intellectual life is not the bastion of objectivity and detachment that our positivist heritage would like to think. Our bias is, moreover, most likely to show itself in the human sciences, for at this point we most want to justify our own moral systems.

It comes as no surprise to a Christian viewpoint, therefore, that Mead's discoveries have come under such questioning. Commentators who wish to throw doubt on Fu'apua'a Fa'amu's testimony, or on Freeman's conclusions, because of their personal social position, must equally take into account Mead's own sexual promiscuity. It may well be no coincidence that the theory she developed was one which justified sexual licence, and declared the moral restrictions of her Western society to be (unnecessarily harsh) human constructs.

If Mead was wrong, we have been sold a personally and socially damaging lie. We trusted, and were encouraged to trust, views which were based on highly questionable data, which should not have taken several decades and a public attack to uncover.[24] Mead's openly promoted views should have been subjected to a scrutiny proportional to the public emphasis she gave them, and we can ask questions about the self-justificatory nature of the academic community that did not do so. At the end of the day, academic discourse cannot hold itself completely aloof from responsibility to the people who are affected by it.

ENDNOTES
1   See James E. Côté, *Adolescent Storm and Stress: An Evaluation of the Mead-Freeman Controversy*, Lawrence Erlbaum Associates, Publishers, Hillsdale, New Jersey, 1994.
2   Margaret Mead, *Coming of Age in Samoa: A Study of Adolescence and Sex in Primitive Societies*, Penguin Books, Harmondsworth, 1928.
3   Forward, in *ibid.*, p. 6.
4   Derek Freeman, *Paradigms in Collision*, Research School of Pacific Studies, ANU, 1992, pp. 3-4.
5   *Ibid.*, p. 16.
6   *Ibid.*, p. 16.
7   *Ibid.*, p. 17.
8   Derek Freeman, *Margaret Mead and Samoa: the Making and Unmaking of an Anthropological Myth*, Harvard University Press, Cambridge, Mass., 1983.

9   Fa'apua'a Fa'amu was by that time an elderly lady who gave testimony on television and whose testimony has since been given in a sworn deposition.

10   Côté, *op. cit.*, p. 28; also see Nicole J. Grant, 'From Margaret Mead's field notes: what counted as "sex" in Samoa?', *American Anthropologist*, 1995, *97*, 678-682, p. 681.

11   See 'Ungodly row over Heretic', and 'Question of belief as writer, director split over Heretic', *Sydney Morning Herald*, 2/4/96; 'Fighting white males', *Sydney Morning Herald*, 6/4/96; 'Some like it hot ... but I don't', and 'Heretic brawl, Act 2: the plot thickens', *Sydney Morning Herald*, 9/4/96; and many other newspaper articles around this time.

12   'Sex, lies and anthropology', *Good Weekend*, 9/3/96.

13   Thomas Kuhn, *The Structure of Scientific Revolutions*, The University of Chicago Press, Chicago, 1962, second edition enlarged 1970. Kuhn's work created a furor of discussion— partly becuse he did not define 'paradigm' strictly himself—and it has become obvious that real life does not fit into neat paradigms, one succeeding the other. Nevertheless, the word remains useful as a general term for the framework of assumptions that lies behind a person's specific work.

14   Theodore Schwartz, in Ivan Brady (ed.), 'Speaking in the name of the real: Freeman and Mead on Samoa', *American Anthropologist*, 1983, *85*, 908-947, p. 920.

15   Côté, *op. cit.*, p. 28.

16   A *matai* is a titled family head, or chief. *Ibid.*, pp. 5-6.

17   That this is common is the argument of Michael Medved in his study *Hollywood vs America*, Harper Perennial, New York, 1992. Medved argues that the film makers of Hollywood have not been motivated by art, integrity or even money but by a desire to attack the traditional values of family life in the American culture. From his perspective, the inclusion of the anthropological debate inside the film *Circle of Friends* would be typical of the use of films to promote an anti-family, sexually libertarian philosophy of life.

18   Côté, *op. cit.*, p. 48. Holmes has also personally studied Samoan culture.

19   Quoted by Derek Freeman, '"O Rose thou art sick!": a rejoinder to Weiner, Schwartz, Holmes, Shore, and Silverman',

American Anthropologist, 1984, *86*, p. 404.
20   *The Sciences* , 1983, *23*, pp. 14 - 18.
21   Freeman's work was judged "unscientific". While a society could possibly have decided, on evidence, that he was wrong, the fact that he presented arguments based on researched data hardly qualifies for the perjorative "unscientific".
22   Such questions are asked in the philosophy and social studies of science. (Editor's note: introductory books in this area are Alan Chalmers, *What is this thing called science?*, University of Queensland Press, St Lucia, 1976 and *Science and its Fabrication*, Open University Press, Milton Keynes, 1990.) The Mead-Freeman controversy is certainly worthy of a case-study.
23   Lowell Holmes wrote at the time "The Harvard University Press promotion of this book involved virtually every shoddy trick known", adding that if this is the way to present a scientific study he is glad his work remained unnoticed on archive shelves rather than becoming a bestseller. 'A tale of two studies', in Ivan Brady (ed) 'Speaking in the name of the real: Freeman and Mead on Samoa', *American Anthropologist*, 1983, *85*, 908-947, p. 934.
24   Freeman's ideas continue to be criticised in anthropological journals even though it is acknowledged that at least some of the points he made about Mead were worth making. For instance, one writer in an article critising Freeman's way of presenting his argument makes the comment "Unfortunately, Freeman's rhetorial overkill detracts from the valid criticisms he does make about Mead's Samoan research". Mac Marshall, 'The wizard of Oz meets the wicked witch of the East: Freeman, Mead, and ethnographic authority', *American Ethnologist*, 1993, *20*, 604-17, p. 612.

3.
Saul

an unknowing prophet of doom

It takes a great deal of courage to be a social critic. It is much easier to be cynical, witty and humorous than to come out and state bluntly what is wrong with our society. Doing so takes a certain kind of brashness, a willingness to disregard sacred taboos, and a lot of nerve. Canadian writer John Ralston Saul appears to have all of these.

Saul is in many ways a frustrating writer to read—and a sentence-by-sentence analysis could no doubt find many inaccuracies of detail, or over-generalization—but the detail is not what makes him interesting. Saul has a brave, far-reaching thesis about how our modern society came to be, and where it went wrong. For its many strengths, and its illuminating weaknesses, it is a thesis worth reviewing.

Saul is a Canadian writer of growing international recognition. He has a PhD in history from Kings College (London). He has worked in business in both France and Canada and has several novels published internationally. In a sense, however, Saul the person is not important, for it might be thought that any intelligent person could have made the social critique Saul has. Nonetheless, millions of intelligent people have not, and this is part of Saul's critique. For the intelligent people have accepted the Enlightenment dogma of rationality, and thought that this was all they needed. Saul disagrees. Our society is not in trouble because of a failure to be rational, he asserts; the major problems of our society have been created by rational people making rational decisions. The problem is that rationality is not enough. Saul points out what has been tragically demonstrated by the modern world: right decisions are not the same as rational ones.

Saul sees that rationality and morality cannot be arbitrarily separated. I agree with Saul, and yet I am constantly frustrated because he has left out an essential part of the picture. Although Saul has seen so much clearly, he has not yet seen that there is an indissoluble link not just between morality and rationality, but between theology, morality and rationality. Because of creation, many of our basic and important concepts can be put forward as self-evident—for instance, utilitarianism in ethics, empiricism in knowledge, and rationality in decision-making. Yet what Saul, and his Enlightenment predecessors, failed to realise is that none of them has a basis apart from the God who created them; and an understanding of their use and abuse only comes from an understanding of the biblical revelation's explanation of their distortion brought about by sin.

An introduction to John Ralston Saul

This article is not a book review, but it is primarily through his books that Saul has launched his ideas.

Three in particular have brought him international fame: *Voltaire's Bastards: The Dictatorship of Reason in the West* (Penguin 1992); *The Doubter's Companion: A Dictionary of Aggressive Common Sense* (Penguin 1995); and *The Unconscious Civilization* (Penguin 1997).

In his internationally best-selling *Voltaire's Bastards*, Saul spells out his basic contention concerning the disastrous consequences of the Age of Reason. *The Doubter's Companion* is a dictionary. Under a range of alphabetically organized topics, Saul provides a counter-cultural way of viewing the world. It is humorous and challenging, as it takes a contrary view on most topics. It is a quicker but less sustained way into the same arguments as *Voltaire's Bastards*. *The Unconscious Civilization* is the published version of the Massey Lectures, broadcast by the Canadian Broadcasting Corporation in 1995. In this, Saul challenges the prominence of economics in democracy. The corporatist world, he argues, is the real enemy of the individual and democracy.

✣

Saul is a questioner and doubter of the present world order. He does not come with packaged answers, or even answers at all. His role is to be the worrying questioner, the loyal opposition, asking the difficult, embarrassing, even inconvenient questions. His is the voice of the small boy who declared that the emperor was wearing no clothes.

In a radio interview with Scott London, Saul explained his approach:

> I'm not in the business of suggesting solutions, by the way. I don't belong to the Platonic tradition, I belong to the Socratic tradition.[1]

Socrates, he said, was an 'oral' philosopher: the questioner, obsessed by ethics, searching for truth without expecting to find it, and a democrat, a believer in the qualities of the citizen. Plato, on the other hand, was primarily 'written': he was an answerer of questions, obsessed by power, one who thought himself in possession of the truth and was contemptuous of the citizens. So Socrates was the father of humanism, Plato the father of ideology. But Plato's greatest flaw, according to Saul, is also the secret of his ongoing political success. He managed to marry Homer's inevitability of the Gods and Destiny, to the newly discovered mechanisms of reason (*Unconscious Civilization*, p. 59).

Modelling himself on Socrates, Saul wishes to restore public debate to the people as a believer in participatory democracy. He believes in people, in individual citizens. He would call himself a humanist. He opposes the elitist specialization of power, and especially knowledge, which uses words and language defensively to protect position, rather than to communicate freely with all. As a graduate of McGill and London universities, he could well be accused of being part of the corporate specialization of knowledge that he criticises. He defended himself in a recent radio interview by claiming that his very studies were conducted in an iconoclastic manner:

> I did my PhD out of Kings College London, but I did it on de Gaulle and the reorganization of France, so I spent the whole time in Paris, and I didn't go near the university that I was supposedly a part of, except once a month for maybe two days. I would go back, have terrible arguments, and then leave town again. Certainly, by the time I had finished it, they weren't at all happy with my PhD—I had one of the most violent oral exams in modern history. It was two and a half hours of screaming basically [Laughs]. But the fact is, I stood up for what I believed in and they didn't have the guts to do anything about it.[2]

Saul is not by any means against knowledge; knowledge is his concern. His point is, this is *public* knowledge, and he is spreading it for public debate. He is taking ideas out of the realm of the specialist destroyers of language, to put them back into the realm of the citizen's understanding and participation in debate.

Saul is not easily classifiable as right wing or left wing. He rejects most of the categories by which people are able to quickly analyse and dismiss ideas. The very activity of such classifications is contrary to his whole position. He seems to be anti-rational, as he writes against such things as the 'Dictatorship of Reason in the West', but that would be a false conclusion to draw about him. His objection is not to reason, of which he uses a lot, but of its isolation from other human qualities. There are at least six qualities he cites as equally important: "common sense, creativity, ethics, intuition, memory, and reason".

Reason may function well as one of them, but reason (or any of them) taken in isolation fails badly. This is his accusation against Voltaire's offspring.

Voltaire is one of Saul's heroes (although he hates the category of hero). Through the spread of knowledge—by the asking of hard questions, by his refusal to be overpowered by the structures of his own day—Voltaire attacked the vested interests and power structures of the aristocracy and church. He relished the importance of reason as a tool for conducting the affairs of humanity. Yet Voltaire was not arguing for reason in isolation. He was not ignoring ethics or common sense. It was his intellectual children, his illegitimate children, who so elevated reason as to make it finally unreasonable.

The thesis

Saul states his basic thesis in *Voltaire's Bastards*. Reason, to the Enlightenment figures such as Voltaire, promised to liberate them from the arbitrary power of the monarchy and the church. Yet detached from any ethical humanism, reason has in this century become a new religion of state-sanctioned violence and dictatorial power. This religion is certainly no better—and in its efficiency considerably worse—than the things that the Enlightenment was revolting against. Reason alone has led to violence and oppression in politics, and to top-heavy bureaucracy in management. Without ethics, it has not only become unethical, it has become unworkable as well.

Saul says we are now in the dotage of the Age of

Reason. It was a great and liberating age, one that we had to pass through.

> Since the 1620's, if not the 1530's, we seem to have merely been fiddling with details or rather, shifting from side to side to disguise the fact that we have taken in that long period but one clear step—away, that is, from the divine revelation and absolute power of church and state.
>
> That very real struggle against superstition and arbitrary power was won with the use of reason and of scepticism (*Voltaire*, p.15).

However, the original assumption that reason "was a moral force" (*Voltaire*, p. 16), has slowly been destroyed, even if we could not at first bring ourselves to abandon this easy conviction. The wars of the twentieth century were not the irrational acts of madmen, but the rational acts of immoral or amoral men.

> The Age of Reason has turned out to be the Age of Structure; a time when in the absence of purpose, the drive for power as a value in itself has become the principal indicator of social approval (*Voltaire* p. 16).

For a good half century now it has been easy to say of our society that Christianity is dead and the psychiatrist is the new priest. But that is true only if you take a fairly shallow view of civilization. In reality, we are today in the midst of a theology of pure power—power born of structure, not of dynasty or arms. The new holy trinity is organization, technology and information. The new priest is the technocrat—the man who understands the organization, makes the use of the technology and controls the access to information, which is a compendium of 'facts' (*Voltaire*, p. 22).

The Age of Reason has now become a tyranny from which we need release. Where it went wrong was where it was strongest: reason. Reason released from its context of morality, humanity, memory and common sense became the structural monster that has created so many of our twentieth-century woes. Saul describes the new dictatorship that reason has created. The seminaries to train the priesthood are the secular universities offering their Master of Business Administration degrees. The father of this abuse of education and learning was the efficiency expert F. W. Taylor (1856-1915) who was the pioneer of scientific management, and the founding school was Harvard.

From this concentration on rational management and control, the economists, social engineers and ruling elites spread—not only into the Western democracies, but with equal proficiency and efficiency into Nazi Germany, Fascist Italy and Communist Russia and China. This was not only the methodology of Mussolini and Hitler, but also Stalin and Mao. It is not just a problem for heads of state, but for the way our whole society is run. The people in power are now the technologists—the people who can *do* things. That is rational. The trouble is, the technologist only knows what he can do and how to go about doing it; he has no criteria to tell him whether it is a good thing to do. In fact, in his categories, 'good' is the same as 'rational'. The technologist will hire himself out to whomever will pay. Now, ruled by reason, morality is a foreign and unhelpful concept to him.

> One reason that he is unable to recognize the necessary relationship between power and morality is that moral traditions are the product of civilization and he has little knowledge of his own civilization (*Voltaire*, p. 110).

Saul chronicles for us the devastating consequences of separating reason from its moorings in society, civilization and morality. He illustrates the ultimately futile and counter-productive attempts to make policies on the basis of technology, without knowing where we are going or what we are trying to achieve. He gives a detailed account of the arms race, which is such a *rational* response for our world economy, but at the same time so completely counterproductive to humanity, and even our own military interests.

Yet reason, when instituted into our society as the sole arbiter of life and meaning, cannot see its way out of its own tyranny. Those who come to power by scepticism, cannot be sceptical of their own use of power without reducing everything to a world-weary cynicism. A perfect example of this is Sir Humphrey Appleby of the *Yes Minister* TV shows. The reason for government is, in the end, the maintenance of the public service.

This 'corporatism' is also reflected in knowledge

structures. Who has the right to 'know' things? Not the average person, any more. Instead of the open, reasoned, common sense, moral intercourse of individual citizens, we have devised the division of labour into fiefdoms of exclusive knowledge and power. These specialized disciplines are unable to communicate with the public because of their specialist jargon, developed to protect their expertise and secrets. They are also unable to communicate with each other, for each has learnt to defend its own territory. The distortion of language is one of the sad reflections of a reason-controlled 'corporatism'.

The result of this exclusivity is that polymaths and grand organizing theorists are now excluded from any position in debate within our society. Each discipline rejects the outside 'amateur' as a threat. The amateur, by definition almost, does not know what he is talking about, especially when he does not use the right forms of language or chooses to speak in terms that the citizenry may be able to understand.

John Ralston Saul is just such an outsider. He writes of economics and art, of politics and religion, of literature and technology, of administration and philosophy. Throughout it, he is an historian. Putting it simply, and not in his words, his case is that the separation of reason from its cultural roots in morality has not only lead to immorality being made more logical, reasonable and efficient, but has also undermined reason and its discourse in society at large.

What is the value of Saul's work?
It is multidisciplinary
The over-specialization of knowledge has been a concern expressed, especially around universities, for many years. Multidisciplinary and interdisciplinary studies have been attempted many times. John Ralston Saul is only one example of many who 'paint the large picture'. Within the university where I worked for over twenty years there has been a long tradition of requiring undergraduates to undertake some courses outside their primary degree. The 'general studies' programmes have tried to introduce the scientific mind to the humanities, and the humanities to the scientists and technologists.

Yet John Ralston Saul has raised more fundamental questions than can be answered by undertaking a simple introductory course on creative writing, or computer technology. It is the question of whether there is a University at all any more. Should our institutions rather be called a Multiversities (*Voltaire*, p. 476)? The very name of 'university' suggests there is still a unified framework that unites all the separate disciplines and minds—yet this is simply no longer true. There is now no common canon of knowledge that can be said to unify our understanding, and should be passed on to the next generation as knowledge.[3]

Consequently there is great difficulty in being taken seriously if one raises the larger questions of life and its meaning. Every specialist finds fault as you travel near their speciality. There is too much information for any real polymath to master. So without some unifying theory, philosophy or culture, we are left to flounder. We gather more information in every discipline, but no longer know why we are gaining it or what we should do with it. The atom bomb is a classic example of the problem of specialized knowledge, without any moral or cultural constraints. That our modern technicians and scientists can do something, is no reason that they *should*. Yet woe betide anyone who raises doubt about the value of new discoveries or endless research. Where in our society can we raise the question of 'should' or harder still 'should not'?

Whether we agree or disagree with Saul, it is very important that we have literature which respects the larger issues of life and will not be bullied by specialists into silence.

It asks the hard questions

It is also valuable to see humanists facing the hard questions that they have been ducking for so long. In 1963, Penguin Books published two volumes: *Objections to Christian Belief* and *Objections to Humanism*. Each book was to be written by the believers, not the adversaries—but it was hardly fair. Christianity has no shortage of variant believers who with honesty and candour can point out its weaknesses. Yet in those days of high humanist orthodoxy, the objections to Humanism were not to be expressed. However today the modernist world is challenged by postmodernity, and the confidence in reason of a previous generation of humanists is evaporating. Reason alone does not provide morality. It was the lie that men such as

Bertrand Russell believed, lived and propagated.[4] It does not provide a culture or a civilization.

John Ralston Saul places a real challenge before the humanist assumptions of superiority. We still hear the slowly receding echoes of Voltaire and his followers, who have told us endlessly that religion causes war, while witnessing the most violent war-filled century—wars that come out of the atheistic philosophies of Nietzsche and Marx. We have seen the creation of an international arms race coming out of rationalistic economics. We have seen the wholesale devaluing of human life, springing out of their amoral rejection of personal ethics.

Now at last, on some level, there is an openness to the possibility that there may have been some mistake. Like the Pope apologizing for the Inquisition, it seems too little too late. Nonetheless, it is there in Saul's book. He is not saying anything more than Christians have been saying for some time; but it is now being said by a non-Christian. Saul is willing to see that all is not well with the world.

There are any number of disastrous failures of our culture in the Western world that we have not been willing to face up to. We live under the myth of democratic government, but it is the legal specialists, the judges, who are now the legislators rather than the elected representatives. We as people are less free than we have ever been. The great desire of Jefferson for life, liberty and the pursuit of happiness has been reduced to the pursuit of pleasures. 'Happiness' has been redefined since Jefferson's day to something that he would oppose, namely the self-centred pursuit of personal hedonism.

The failure of rationality detached from morality: a case-study

It is this willingness to face the failure of reason to provide morality which makes Saul's hypotheses so attractive. Gone is the pretence that utilitarianism—the view that what works best, is best—could come up with an ethic worth living. Utilitarianism is simply a structural approach to problems. At best it gives us a temporary trial of what may turn out for the good, until more evidence persuades us otherwise. Yet the trial never defines the good in a measurable fashion, and the detrimental consequences of the trial are never part of the equation.

Coincidentally, another recently-published book provides a perfect case-study of Saul's thesis: Anne Coombs' *Sex and Anarchy: the Life and Death of the Sydney Push*.[5] This book tells the story of the avant-guard movement known as 'the Sydney Push', which scandalised 'polite' Sydney society earlier this century, with its Bloomsbury-like disregard of traditional values.[6] The great Socratic father of this movement, Professor John Anderson, was even, like Socrates, accused of corrupting the morals of the youth of the city. This, of course, was regarded as laughable and ridiculous by those with corrupt morals, and it gave martyr status to the great 'philosophic' tradition. However the rationalistic atheism of the Andersonian system unleashed a whirlwind of anarchy and sexual abuse, that is breathtaking in its hypocrisy and horror. The systematic exploitation of young women, for the insatiable satisfaction of men, was appalling—and finally came to be seen as such by the women concerned. There was a great promise of freedom and equality, but it was just the old bondage and slavery in a new rationalistic and intellectually self-justifying clothing. In the 1970s when, under the influence of feminism, some 'women's only' meetings started in the home of Jane Gardiner, Anne Coombs reports:

> There was a stirring of resentment among many Push women. Adding a peculiar potent flavour to this resentment for many of them was the recognition that not only had they not been treated equally but they had also been sexually hoodwinked. Free sex had not always been great sex and they'd spent years blaming themselves. It was a bitter herb (p. 270).

Gardiner says, "Those meetings were the death knell of the Push. The women were no longer so impressed by the men and were prepared to go off and do things their own way".

Whether it is intentional or not, the whole of Anne Coombs's book is a biting indictment on the heartless, ruthless decadence of rationalism separated from a context of morality. It is an illustration in microcosm of the argument of John Ralston Saul.

What is defective in Saul's work?

Given all this agreement with the writings of John

Ralston Saul, it may be surprising to hear that basically I consider his whole argument flawed. First, however, some minor points of criticism.

His use of specialists

There is not much to be gained by complaining about minor inaccuracies—of which, admittedly, there are quite a few—for Saul's writing is not of the character which can be fairly criticized by minor errors. There is especially not much point criticizing this literature from within specialist knowledge, for the whole nature of specialist knowledge is being questioned and challenged.

However, there is some inconsistency in the specialists Saul uses to help him write his books. He does not deny the usefulness of expert knowledge in its place, and at the back of *Voltaire's Bastards* he lists the names of experts who have advised him on various areas. In the small area of life I occupy, however, I noticed that his sample of 'religious experts' was very biased, and that this bias is reflected in his books.

It is probably because of this that Saul's concern for memory, which is so admirable in an historian, and so important for a community, is not matched by the significance he gives to the Reformation. Saul recounts how superstition and arbitrary power were the enemies with which Voltaire contended; but fails to mention the Roman Catholic nature of the Paris that massacred Protestants two hundred years before Voltaire's triumphal entry. That the enlightened Age of Reason had great affect upon the considerations of freedom in

Western thought is not to be denied; but the Reformation can hardly be so blithely ignored without some explanation. It appears that Saul has not understood the protest of Protestantism and still views Christianity and Roman Catholicism as synonymous. Repeatedly he refers to the eating and drinking of Christ's flesh and blood, as if this Roman Catholic understanding had never been challenged by anyone.

Furthermore, Saul does not seem to have freed himself from the Age of Reason when considering religion. In his view Christianity, like all religion, is a matter of fear, magic and ritual. It is humanity searching in order to find our way to immortality. It is superstitious myth, to help humanity discover its way out of fear. Such an uneducated prejudice is unbecoming to a writer who wishes to deal with the large issues of life.

He does not understand biblical Christianity

With such a view on religion, it is not surprising that Saul does not understand biblical Christianity. The Bible is spoken of only in terms of myths and superstition. The only part of the Bible he tries to assess is the book of Revelation (which he consistently misnames 'Revelations'). Saul's evaluation of the book of Revelation cannot be ignored, for he claims that it played an important part in transforming the true teaching of Jesus into something that made it possible that "governments and administrators of formal religion were able to gain control over Christ's language" (*Voltaire*, p. 542). He describes the book of Revelation as:

pages of raving. These include the entire pagan, superstitious, dark tradition which dominated the Western barbarian imagination until the arrival of Christianity (*Voltaire*, p. 542).

... adding:

> Pagan cults were often difficult for those in power to deform or manipulate because they combined strict public ritual with a narrow set of ironclad rules. Paul and his Epistles are often blamed for Christianity's strange tangents. But his contributions were merely politics and policy. John's Revelations altered the nature of the Christian ethic. It blew the Christian message so wide open that any extreme action, good or evil, could be justified—self-sacrifice, martyrdom, purity, devotion and concern for others had no greater purchase in Christ's official Testament than did racism, violence or absolutism of any sort. Whoever wrote John's text was consciously or unconsciously in the service of organized authority (*Voltaire*, p. 543).

This view, not just of Revelation, but also Paul and the rest of the New Testament—especially the teachings of Jesus—is frankly incredible. It can only lead me to conclude that either Saul has read a different Bible from the one normally published, or he has not read it at all!

Maybe my criticisms could be viewed as the carping of yet another specialist corporatism man, threatened by the truth taught by an amateur. I would maintain, however, that the Bible is not a specialist book—it is given by

God to be the people's book. Biblical Christianity is not an arcane speciality; it is openly accessible to public understanding. The Bible is the 'alternative grand scheme' of everything, which would solve problems Saul describes. Here is the publicly available theory of life, the universe and meaning, that resolves the tensions which are created by Enlightenment rationality. However the kind of nonsense Saul writes about the Bible comes out of the ivory towers of specialist corporatist study that he is so quick to criticize in other disciplines.

Saul does not return to where we went wrong

My major disagreement with Saul is this: John Ralston Saul sees that the problem of Voltaire's followers is reason in isolation. Reason needs to stay in touch with morality. However Saul, in line with his Socratic stance of creative doubt without answers, never explains how to keep reason in touch with morality, or where morality comes from or what it is. In fact, apart from a few references to logic, reason is not explained either. Here biblical Christianity would have helped him. For Christianity is not a magical, ritual, fear-driven pursuit of immortality; Christianity provides (amongst other things) a reasonable morality which deals with the reality of human existence.

From time to time Saul recognizes that with the enthronement of reason came the assassination of God. In one radio interview he said,

> I guess what I'm really attacking is the isolation of reason. In other words, the obsession we have in the West with this idea that reason is the great quality.

We've replaced God the Father with reason.

While he sees this clearly, he misunderstands the Bible and the implications of replacing God the Father with reason. In the same interview he said:

> Let me take us back to the question, 'How is knowledge perceived in the West?' The original founding Judeo-Christian myth has two innocents being convinced to eat the apple of knowledge by the devil. So from the very beginning of society the definition of knowledge by those who have power (the people who wrote those books) was that innocence is good, knowledge is evil and comes from the devil, and only the devil would spread knowledge. It's not simply the eating of the apple, the getting of knowledge, it's the spreading of knowledge—letting the secret of knowledge out. It sounds like the 20th century, doesn't it? It sounds like specialist elites holding on to their knowledge.[7]

It is not just that Saul gets the biblical details wrong by omitting the nature of the knowledge. In doing this, he actually misses the point of the whole Genesis account. But the problem is worse, for the point that he misses is, in fact, the Bible's alternative explanation to the failure of isolated reason, that would enhance his whole thesis.

The tree in the Genesis account is the tree of the knowledge of good and evil. It is one of the *devil's* lies that he is the dispenser of knowledge, while God is the authoritarian censor. God is truth, just as the devil is the liar. The devil's temptation was exactly that in to which the Age of Reason fell, namely to know good and evil independently of God. God was not, and never has been in the Bible, opposed to reason or knowledge. He is always opposed to the arrogance of humans, who believe that they can acquire such knowledge independently of him, so that they will be able to rule their own affairs without him.

That was the humanist/secularist dream—the dream that Saul has so tellingly portrayed as a nightmare. It is, in fact, just the kind of nightmare that the Bible predicts. Our morality cannot be divorced from our reasoning, neither in its foundation nor in its results. Moreover, neither reason nor morality can be divorced from our maker. With relationship with God we have a *basis* for both reason and morality—a basis that can keep all in unity and harmony, such that we can truly have a University.

✢

It is time for rationalists to recognise that their answers have not worked. Saul, for all his faults, is doing the world a great service in pointing this out so loudly. When an entire culture is going disastrously the wrong way, it takes a very loud voice to turn it back. Saul is shouting at the top of his voice, and we can hope that rationalists might actually listen to reason and see that the Enlightenment experiment has turned out horribly. However, given the momentum that Enlightenment rationalism has gained—and the social chaos it has created—one voice will hardly be enough. Maybe more humanists will see the flaws in their own doctrine, and join this kind of protest. How much more should Christians—who, after all, have had the information to see it all along—protest? Christianity has taken a public beating in the last two hundred years, and many Christians have sadly lost their nerve, or capitulated to the very Enlightenment reasoning which is now collapsing around their ears. The Bible has always warned of the consequences of trying to work rationally without the light of God; now those consequences are so obvious, it is time for Christians to have boldness in pointing them out.

The Bible is a very profound book, if only we would listen to it. This brings us to the final challenge: it is time for atheists to deal with biblical Christianity, not the foolish nonsense created by unbiblical scholars. If someone can be as insightful as Saul in analyzing society, surely he can take the time to deal with the real issues of Christianity, not imagined ones. It is neither rational, nor moral, to do otherwise.

John Ralston Saul is a man with half the truth, which is doing a whole lot better than most. We could do with more of his kind of courageous critique, stating the big questions instead of being bogged down in minutiae. It is only then that we can start to get our priorities around the right way, where expertise serves the people instead of obscuring knowledge. To do that properly, however, we need to know what the priorities are; and reason alone cannot tell us that. There *are* big answers available; let us not stop with the questions.

ENDNOTES

1   This interview was adapted from the Insight & Outlook radio series, hosted by Scott London. Copyright 1996 by Scott London. www.west.net/~insight/london.

2   *Ibid*.

3   For instance, James W. Sire, *The Universe Next Door*, IVP, London, 1988, argues that each person living next door occupies a different 'world view' or intellectual universe.

4   See 'Peace I did not find' in this volume.

5   Viking, Sydney, 1996.

6   For a review of Anne Coombes' *Sex and Anarchy: the Life and Death of the Sydney Push* see Rory Shiner, 'The Sydney Push', *kategoria*, 2003, 29, pp.7-19.

7   Interview with Scott London, *op. cit*.

4.
Happiness on trial
has utilitarianism failed?

*T*HE BASIC ETHICAL SYSTEM of modern western liberal democracies is utilitarianism. It is an old system which is taken up by ruling bodies because of its practicality and its ability to draw conclusions without recourse to a higher metaphysical authority, such as God. Its standard expression, found in philosophers from ancient Greece to imperial Britain, is that the best course of action—the morally correct thing to do—is whatever produces the most happiness for the most people.

Briefly, utilitarianism is an ethical theory that looks to the results of an action to determine its moral worth. In this philosophy, actions are not *intrinsically* right or wrong. Nor are they to be evaluated against some authority's edict. That is, any particular action—for instance, theft—is not wrong because there is something inherently evil about the concept, nor because a deity has decreed it. Rather, it is wrong because it fails to improve the lot of humanity. It is wrong because it hurts someone, and it is wrong because it is detrimental to society. Bertrand Russell spoke as a utilitarian when he discussed ethical codes in these terms: "[T]he question whether a code is good or bad is the same as the question whether or not it promotes human happiness."[1] Utilitarianism is sometimes referred to as the 'Happiness Theory'.

The method of utilitarianism is rational, empirical and democratic. It is rational because only reason determines the outcome; it is not based on some moral instinct, but on a measured decision about what will, objectively, improve people's lives. It is empirical because utilitarian decisions are open to the evaluation of the *evidence* that can be measured. It is democratic because there is no respecting of vested interests and special cases. Again note Bertrand Russell:

> Those who have a scientific outlook on human behaviour, moreover, find it impossible to label any action as 'sin'; they realise that what we do has its origin in our heredity, our education, and our environment, and that it is by control of these causes rather than by denunciation, that conduct injurious to society is to be prevented.[2]

Although Western democracies all share something of a leftover Christian ethic, utilitarianism is the *modus operandi* of ethical debate today. It is not a theory wholly opposed to Christianity, for Christians believe in a creator God whose moral choices will produce the good life, and whose good life promotes happiness and opposes pain. It was therefore only a small shift for Enlightenment moralists to move society from Christian to utilitarian ethics. Yet since the days of Jeremy Bentham, James Mill, J. S. Mill and Bertrand Russell, utilitarianism has been the preferred choice of *anti-Christian* ethicists. It has been a welcome alternative to a

Christian doctrine of morality, favoured by those who oppose Christian doctrine in general.

This is probably because utilitarianism rejects God's divine prerogative of deciding what is right or wrong in his world. It dismisses relationship with God as the motivation and teacher of morality. It renounces the words, commands and declarations of God as a basis of ethical knowledge. It ignores the inherent rightness or wrongness of an action in favour of looking to the outcomes of actions. It assumes that human well-being or happiness is the ultimate good, regardless of God.

Utilitarianism under scrutiny

But one need not be a Christian to find utilitarianism wanting as a moral philosophy. Ever since utilitarianism has become the dominant ethical basis of Western society, it has been under critical attack. There is, and has been, great debate and disagreement about the theory. For instance, some philosophers claim that every *action* should be evaluated independently, while others argue that *rules* have a utility that will override particular situations. Should each example of murder be examined to see if it really did decrease the well-being of humanity, or is it more ethical to agree that 'murder is wrong' is a rule that should be institutionalised for the well-being of humanity? Added to this, there has never been much agreement on how to *measure* the outcomes, especially for something as vague as 'well-being'.

The debates about measurement are not so much about the difficulties of measuring quality of life, but *whose* life to measure. Should it be the life of the upper class only? Hardly, since utilitarianism rests on democracy—although evaluation of the happiness created by the art gallery compared to the Rugby League competition brings class issues into play. More subtly, should the measurement be of the happiness of the whole, or of each individual within the whole? Egoists might argue that if we concern ourselves with the happiness of each individual, the whole will look after itself. Non-egoists think that the whole will be able to maximise happiness only if certain individuals miss out on some of their own choices of happiness. Who decides such issues? And how much unhappiness will an individual be required to endure for the well-being of the whole?

The definition of 'well-being' also has great difficulties. Some utilitarians are hedonists, believing that happiness is a matter of experiencing feelings of pleasure; others (such as the ancient utilitarians, the Epicureans) have a more sombre approach, choosing the absence of trouble as the way to optimise happiness.

Of all the difficulties of utilitarianism, the question of its ethical *motivation* is possibly the greatest. Utilitarianism fails to answer the big question of ethics—'why?'. Why should I behave in any way other than what I want to? If utilitarianism is just describing why I do behave in the way that I do, rather than telling me *what* to do, then ethics is just psychology. If, on the other hand, utilitarianism is telling us how we *should* or *ought* to behave, it fails to give reasons for being so prescriptive. There is no ultimate answer as to why we should deny our own interests for the benefit of anyone else, and why we should be concerned for the good of the whole. If the argument is simply that it is in my best interests to benefit the whole, then (apart from reducing ethics to a rather selfish level) it cannot be proven.

On a range of levels, utilitarianism has deep problems which have never been resolved. Nonetheless, it continues as the dominant form of ethics in Western society. Most ethical questions are still decided on the utilitarian basis of 'whom will it benefit?', regardless of the deep inconsistencies such a decision will embrace.

How can we test utilitarianism?

While there is a wealth of philosophical literature examining the technical weaknesses in utilitarianism as a moral philosophy, we do not need to rely on that to assess it for ourselves. The test for whether utilitarianism works as a moral philosophy is to look at the results—which we are now easily able to do, given the immense amount of social data routinely collated and made available. Are the decisions based on utilitarian ideals actually bringing good to the majority in our society? And if they are not, is the expected utilitarian response—that is, to rescind that decision and try something else—being put into action?

A comparison of Bertrand Russell's essay *Our Sexual Ethics* (1936) with the recent Australian government report *To Have and to Hold: Strategies to Strengthen Marriage and Relationships* (1998) provides a test-case for utilitarianism in action in the area of personal relationships.[3]

Certain ethical changes have been made in our social structure over the last several decades (commonly called 'the sexual revolution'), and now we have the chance to see whether they worked—whether they did, as was claimed at the time, lead to a better society and more happiness for individuals.

Russell's sexual revolution

The basis of Bertrand Russell's proposed sexual revolution was the utilitarian theory of ethics. The time was past, he considered, for church morality. It was not helping anyone—on the contrary, it was actually harming people, for their subconscious conditioning was warring with their natural impulses. It was a bad system of morality. It did not promote human happiness.

On this basis, Bertrand Russell spelled out a new sexual morality for society. Instead of one based on the archaic and (in his view) false authority of Christianity, there should be a new sexual ethic which took seriously the reality of human impulses and organised society in a way that would be best for everyone. His predictions for future sexual ethics have proved uncannily accurate. What Russell first published in 1936 is astoundingly familiar to the modern Western reader at the end of the 1990s.

For instance, consider the four specific changes that Russell suggested were necessary for society:

> In the first place, it is undesirable, both physiologically and educationally, that women should have children before the age of 20. Our ethics should,

therefore, be such as to make this a rare occurrence.

In the second place, it is unlikely that a person without previous sexual experience, whether man or woman, will be able to distinguish between mere physical attraction and the sort of congeniality that is necessary in order to make marriage a success. Moreover, economic causes compel men, as a rule, to postpone marriage, and it is neither likely that they will remain chaste in the years from 20 to 30, nor desirable psychologically that they should do so; but it is much better that, if they have temporary relations, that they should not be with professionals, but with girls of their own class, whose motive is affection rather than money. For both these reasons, young people should have considerable freedom as long as children are avoided.

In the third place, divorce should be possible without blame to either party, and should not be regarded as in any way disgraceful. A childless marriage should be terminable at the wish of one of the partners, and any marriage should be terminable by mutual consent —a year's notice being necessary in either case. Divorce should, of course, be possible on a number of other grounds—insanity, desertion, cruelty, and so on; but mutual consent should be the most usual ground.

In the fourth place, everything possible should be done to free sexual relations from economic taint. At present, wives, just as much as prostitutes, live by the sale of their sexual charms; and even in temporary free relations the man is usually expected to bear all the joint expenses. The result is that there is sordid entanglement of money with sex, and that women's motives not infrequently have a mercenary element. Sex, even when blessed by the church, ought not to be a profession. It is right that a woman should be paid for housekeeping or cooking or the care of the children, but not merely for having sexual relations with a man. Nor should a woman who was once loved and been loved by a man be able to live ever after on alimony when his love and hers have ceased. A woman like a man should work for her living, and an idle wife is no more intrinsically worthy of respect than a gigolo (pp. 122-3).

Does this sound familiar? Russell was a prophet of the 1960s sexual revolution, 30 years ahead of his time. All of his hopes have been realised: delayed marriage and sexual freedom before marriage; cohabitation on the way to marriage; no-fault divorce after 12 months separation. Perhaps even more interesting, however, is Russell's prediction that sexual freedom for women must come at the price of (or in Russell's view, with the added benefit of) both women working and the destruction of the traditional family structure: "If women are to have sexual freedom, fathers must fade out, and wives must no longer expect to be supported by their husbands. This may come about in time, but it will be a profound social change, and its effects, for good or ill, are incalculable" (pp. 121-2).[4]

It was good, not ill, that Russell was expecting. These changes would make society happier and freer, and the lives of adults would be more honest, easier and generally more pleasurable. The important thing was that ethics should be based on what humans are like, and what really makes them happy, not on some traditional view of 'sin' with no real existence in human nature.

> In seeking a new ethic of sexual behaviour, therefore, we must not ourselves be dominated by the ancient irrational passions which gave rise to the old ethic, though we should recognise that they may, by accident, have led to some sound maxims, and that, since they still exist, though perhaps in a weakened form, they are still among the data of our problem. What we have to do positively is to ask ourselves what moral rules are most likely to promote human happiness, remembering always that, whatever the rules may be, they are not likely to be observed. That is to say, we have to consider the effect which the rules will in fact have, not that which they would have if they were completely effective (p. 125).

Russell proposed a utilitarian sexual experiment for Western society. Only when the effects were tested, could it be seen how clearly superior this new sexual ethic was. Divorce would be made easy; the patriarchal family could easily be done away with; the State could support children, and marriage would become unfashionable, except among the "rich and the religious". But first these things needed to be tried in practice: "Much ground remains to be covered by a complete sexual ethic, but I do not think we can say anything very positive until we have more experience, both of the effects of various systems and of the changes resulting from a rational education in matters of sex" (p. 126).

The results of the experiment

Fortunately for social experimenters, we can now test the success of Russell's recommendations. The recent Australian government report *To Have and to Hold: Strategies to Strengthen Marriage and Relationships* publishes material on the state of marriage and families in Australia today. Did Russell's (and many other proponents) proposals lead to a better society and more happiness for individuals? It is clear from the outset that the answer is no.

In the preface to the report, the chairman of the committee describes the legislative changes that took place in the early 1970s, culminating in the Family Law Act. Two pillars emerged:

> ... first, the importance of family: and secondly the rights and obligation of spouses both during the marriage and upon its ending. Hence the bill introduced in 1973, upon which subsequent bills were drafted, was based on a series of stated principles, the first of which was that 'a good family law should buttress, rather than undermine, the stability of marriage'. The central importance of marriage was explicitly recognised in section 43 of the Family Law Act. This section provided that, in making any adjudication, the family court must have regard to:

> the need to preserve and protect the institution of marriage as the union of a man and a woman to the exclusion of all others voluntarily entered into for life; the need to give the widest possible protection and assistance to the family as the natural and fundamental group unit of society, particularly while it is responsible for the care and education of dependent children; the need to protect the rights of children and promote their welfare; and the means available for assisting parties to marriage to consider reconciliation or the improvement of their relationship to each other and to the children of the marriage.

This pillar was supported by requirements in both the Marriage Act and the Family Law Act for the provision of funds to marriage education and counselling services. The second pillar is most significant:

> The other pillar of the Family Law Act is reflected in the replacement of the grounds of divorce based on matrimonial fault with a single ground—breakdown of marriage, evidenced by 12 months separation of the parties.

Two decades after the introduction of the Family Law Act, this pillar, the divorce of the parties, remains the predominant operational basis of the legislation (pp. i-ii).

It is clear from the report that the first pillar of the Family Law Act is now seen for the weak rhetoric that it was. The resources of the family law court have been poured into the destruction of families, not their preservation. The real pillar of the legislation is the easy dissolution of the marriage bond. In fact, the easy dissolution of marriage has effectively redefined marriage to mean: "a couple voluntarily entering into a legal co-habitation will not be able to enter into another legal co-habitation until twelve months separation from the first cohabitation". Nobody makes promises in those terms during a wedding service—what they say is "to have and to hold from this day forward, for better and for worse until death us do part".

The words of the contract bear no relationship to the meaning of the contract, thanks to the Family Law Act, because the power of the Act resides in the second pillar; the ease of dissolution. At the time of the Act, many voices were raised expressing this problem, but were overruled because of the difficulty that people were experiencing in a court system which required some demonstration of fault in order to dissolve a marriage. Now, 25 years later, the Federal government has a report recognizing the problems that are emerging from their effective redefinition of marriage.

Statistical evidence

At one level, *To Have and To Hold* is an excellent report and the committee needs to be commended for its work and its willingness to report difficult conclusions honestly. There is a positive emphasis within this committee's work, reflected even in the report's title. Yet, in statistic after statistic, the report reveals the inadequacy of utilitarian sexual ethics.

The report naturally commences with a review of trends in marriage and the family since World War II. It was a period of quite significant change. The number of families with dependent children has decreased; the number of one-parent families has increased, as has the number of children being raised by step-parents. People are marrying less, are doing so at an older age and more frequently cohabiting before marriage. More people are remaining unmarried and, although the rate of remarriage has fallen, by 1992 one in three marriages included at least one partner who had been married previously. Only 57% of weddings in 1994 were celebrated by ministers of religion. The population has instead turned to secular wedding celebrants.

There has been a dramatic increase in divorce, even taking into account the sudden increase caused by the new Family Law Act in the early 1970s. The rate of divorce never returned to the low levels prior to the Family Law Act, and since 1986 has been steadily increasing. The number of children involved in divorce has grown markedly in the past two decades. At the same time, marriages that end in divorce have become briefer. There has been a rise in the proportion of previously married people divorcing again. There is a greater chance of divorce amongst those who remarry, as opposed to those marrying for the first time, unless the reason for remarriage was the death of the first partner. Almost half the children whose mothers divorce have a step-father living in the household within six years.

There has been a dramatic increase in the number

of children born out of wedlock. At the end of World War II just 4% of children were born out of wedlock; in 1995 it was 26.6%. About half ex-nuptial births were to women in *de facto* relationships and about half to unpartnered women. There has been a rise in teenage ex-nuptial pregnancies, although overall a decrease in births to teenage mothers (nuptial and ex-nuptial). There has been a substantial increase of single parent families with dependent children from 6.5% in 1976, to 14.5% in 1996.

The social impact

Even more powerful than the statistics is the examination of the impact of these changes. The authors' summation of the present state of our knowledge leaves little doubt as to what is happening.

- Decades of research have clearly established links between health and well-being and marriage, separation and divorce (p. 27).
- Virtually every study which has analysed mortality rate by marital status shows that the unmarried have higher death rates, a finding confirmed since the 1930's in every country for which accurate health data exists (p. 28).
- Relationship breakdown is one of the major causes of suicide worldwide, and the differential in mortality rates by marital status is huge (p. 31).
- Both perceived physical and mental health have been found to be related to marital status in a way similar to mortality (p. 32).

- Marital distress is an important health hazard for adults and children ... Marital distress leads to depression and reduces immune system functioning in adults (p. 33).
- A large number of studies have shown that divorce has both a short term and long term impact on children. Research also demonstrates that this impact often extends into adult life with consequences for health, family life, educational performance and occupational status (p. 34).
- There is also widespread evidence of increased behavioural problems and delinquency among both boys and girls whose parents have divorced (p. 35).
- Marital disruption has also been implicated in youth depression and suicide, and early sexual activity (p. 36).

A series of other studies indicate that:

- children of divorced parents seem much more susceptible to psychiatric illness;
- alcohol consumption by women whose parents divorced is far higher than women with intact families;
- the incidence of stomach ulcers and colitis is four times higher for men aged 26 whose parents have divorced before the child was five compared to those who have reached 16 years when their parents divorced;
- children of divorce ... have a 50% greater risk of developing asthma, and a 20-30% greater risk of injury; and

- parental divorce can be a factor in longevity (p. 35).

A series of studies which has examined the impact of parental divorce on children have found that the educational performance of children is adversely effected. These studies reveal that:

- the adverse educational effects of divorce can occur in children of any age;
- the chances of attending university decrease for children of divorce; and
- unemployment and employment in low paying jobs is more prevalent for children of divorced parents (p. 37).

Series of studies have confirmed the intergenerational impact of divorce. 25 years after their parents divorce, children continue to suffer the emotional repercussions. The impact of divorce among children is long-lasting and cumulative (p. 39).

Naturally, analysts need to face the complex question of which correlative factors in these summaries are causative, and which ones are resultant. There is also the question of whether some other unidentified factors may give rise to these problems. However, the detailed studies of researchers from around the world, as well as in Australia, led the committee to their damning conclusions about the impacts of change in family life in Australia over the last 25 years.

To begin, family violence is at an unacceptably high level, and seems to have some relationship to the nature of the family structure:

[t]here is ... some evidence that the incidence of conflict is higher in cohabiting relationships ... there are more cohabitants reporting conflicts ... than married ... cohabitants, especially women, seem to tolerate in their partners types of behaviour which marriers consider unacceptable (pp. 46-47).

The incidence of child abuse and neglect also seems related to relationship dysfunction ... a higher proportion of child killers are either stepfathers or the mother's *de facto* or boyfriend ... non-biological parents present 'a disproportionate risk for children, particularly in the early stages of their relationship with the child'. The proportion of suspected killers in *de facto* relationships was 6.5 times higher than for the general population. The study found that 28 per cent of the child killers had become parents when aged 20 years or younger (p. 47).

... family conflict, including violence and abuse, is one of the major factors leading to youth homelessness in Australia (p. 47).

... marriage benefits the health and well-being of individuals, and, conversely ... separation and divorce bring with them elevated risks for both former husbands and wives and their children. The extent to which these findings are accepted by social scientists is reflected in the work of a number of leading researchers. Sara McLanahan, herself a single parent, and professor of sociology at Princeton University, concluded her detailed

> analysis of four major national studies of families ... : "Children who grow up in a household with only one biological parent are worse off, on average, than children who grow up in a household with both of their biological parents, regardless of the parent's race or educational background, regardless of whether the parents are married when the child is born, and regardless of whether the resident parent remarries" (p. 48).

The government committee ends this section with the only way of accounting available: money. Apart from anything else, the breakdown in marriage is costing us.

> Marriage and relationship breakdown is a direct cost to the Commonwealth budget in the form of social security payments, family court costs, legal aid, the child support scheme, and taxation rebates ... These items total $2,771 million per annum. The figure is necessarily conservative. Other costs could be rightfully included in the cost of marriage and relationship breakdown, but it is difficult to separate the components. For example, the expenditure on emergency accommodation and the homeless allowance partly arises from marriage breakdown, but it has not been possible to determine the size of this part (p. 50) ...
>
> A review of the literature indicates that poor health is partly a consequence of marriage and relationship breakdown. The extent of this cost to the nation is immeasurable. It extends not only to physical and mental health, but to the

social pathologies such as child and family abuse. Similarly, absenteeism and low productivity have been linked to relationship problems (pp. 50-51).

The committee comes to this understated conclusion:

> Marriage and family breakdown cost the Australian nation at least $3 billion each year. When all the indirect costs are included, the figure is possibly double. When the personal and emotional trauma involved is added to these figures, the cost to the nation is enormous.
>
> In comparison the Commonwealth Government spends just $3.5 million per annum on preventative marriage and relationship education programs, and $2.05 million on parenting skills training. This is a 1000 fold difference. The imbalance is manifest. It requires correction (p. 51).

Contributing Factors

In the fourth chapter of the report, the committee looks at what causes, or at least contributes to, marriage and relationship breakdowns. Again their work is a summation of the detailed research that has been undertaken in recent years. They report the determinants of marital instability in the following terms:

> In a recent survey of the determinants of marital instability, AIFS researcher, Helen Glezer, found that the premarital experiences contributing most to the risk of marital breakdown are:

- having an ex-nuptial child;
- premarital cohabitation; and
- leaving home at an early age.

According to Glezer:

> Characteristics of those who experienced marital breakdown compared with those who have not, indicate that like those who have cohabited, they tend to have less traditional family values, are more egalitarian about sex roles, value children less and are more individualistic in their family orientation than those who remain married.
>
> ... family background factors such as growing up in a non-religious family, being unhappy at home, leaving home at an early age, and coming from a context of non-traditional family values are associated with both cohabiting prior to marriage and marital dissolution.

A series of studies have identified other demographic and social characteristics that have been shown to contribute to marital instability. These include:

- exposure to divorce as a child;
- having premarital sex; and
- marrying as a teenager (pp. 74-75).

The chapter is stronger when it takes a case study of cohabitation and looks at the factors contributing to marital stability. The numbers of couples living together, both before and as a substitute for marriage, has increased substantially in recent decades. The community now believes that it is beneficial for couples to live together prior to marriage, and expert opinion of the past two decades has commended cohabitation. However more recent social science research points to a connection between cohabitation and marital breakdown. The Australian Institute of Family Studies *Family Formation Project* found that after five years of marriage, 13% of those who had cohabited were divorced, compared to 6% of those who had not cohabited. Ten years later, the proportions were 26% for those who had cohabited and 14% for those who had not. After 20 years it was 56% compared to 27% (pp. 78-79). These findings have been supported by similar studies in Canada, the United Kingdom, the United States and Sweden.

It is not just that cohabiters have a higher risk of subsequent divorce, they also have a less satisfactory relationship:

> Studies have also found couples who cohabit prior to marriage to be significantly lower on measures of marital quality. DeMaries and Lesley hypothesised that cohabiters would score higher on communication and couple adjustment in their study. However they found a negative relationship between cohabitation and satisfaction ... It has also been found that the rate of violence is appreciably higher for cohabiting couples who have lived together for one to ten years than for married couples (pp. 81-82).

The effect on children is not positive either. "Where couples who cohabit have children, research indicates that the children perform at lower levels than children of married couples" (p. 82). Low performance was noted in scholastic achievement, and there was greater drug use, crime and delinquency. The Committee concludes:

> ... marriages preceded by cohabitation show 'lower levels of marital interaction, higher levels of disagreement and instability ... lower levels of commitment to marriage' and higher levels of divorce than marriages without previous cohabitation experience ... in many instances, cohabitation is not a relationship with a future, but one that lasts for a period of time and then ends, either through marriage or dissolution (p. 83).

To summarise, the factors in marital *instability* seem difficult to identify but the determinants of marital *stability* seem a little easier:

> [E]ffective communication and conflict resolution; realistic expectation of marriage; equitable division of labour within family; fertility within marriage; length of marital duration; and religious commitment (p. 85).

Where to now?

This government report would seem to be a utilitarian's dream, but it turns out to be a nightmare. We now have the statistical information, studies, academic analysis and measured results of a social, ethical and legal experiment. For centuries, a marital pattern was taught, legislated and upheld by the social conventions of the day. Now, thanks to the 1960s sexual revolution and the 1970s enactment of it through legislation, we have had 25 years of experimentation with a new way of family living. The government has gathered the evidence concerning the consequences of this change. At every point we can measure so far, the experiment has been a disaster for the well-being and happiness of the community.

If the committee's analysis is correct, then utilitarians ought to have no alternative but to cease the experiment and seek a happier way to organise society, or at least return to the previous form of social organisation. Bertrand Russell admitted this possibility:

> The fundamental difficulty is, of course, the conflict between the impulse to jealousy and the impulse to sexual variety. Neither impulse, it is true, is universal: there are those (though they are few) who are never jealous, there are those (among men as well as among women) whose affections never wander from the chosen partner. If either of these types could be made universal, it would be easy to devise a satisfactory code. It must be admitted, however, that either type can be made more common by conventions designed to that end.[5]

However, the government committee was unable to see what to do or how to do it. Its recommendations fall broadly into two categories. The first is to tidy up the finances. Different marriage counselling organisations have been funded on different bases, and there seems to be some lack of consistency and equity. It is only sensible to sort out such problems.

The second set of recommendations urges that more premarital counselling needs to be given. As with the financial recommendations, nobody could object to this. Evidence is adduced that premarital counselling is effective. However, the one group whom the report indicates are amongst the greatest contributors to marital dissolutions—that is, cohabiters—are the group who would be least helped by any of this premarital counselling. While it is possible to measure the rates of divorce, the even higher rates of dissolution of *de facto* relationships for which premarital counselling is rarely if ever sought, is not taken into account.

There is no doubt that the committee is making right recommendations. However, there is a certain Gilbertian absurdity in these kinds of recommendations, given the scale of the problem. The government alone cannot change a culture which is worldwide and has been developing over the last 150 years.[6] However if the government *is* concerned about the community's well-being, then it could take certain actions that would help create a climate in which the social experiment could be reversed. We encourage governments to act on other issues, such as smoking, where the actions of an individual are to the detriment of the community. Ought we not request similar action in areas such as *de facto* marriages where the evidence of their harmful effects is now available? And might not some pressure be brought upon the advocates of these kinds of relationships (such as some parts of the mass media) to correct the false information being disseminated about the nature of sexuality and relational happiness?

One clearly beneficial action which is unlikely to reach any public agenda, is that the government could support the religious cultures of the majority of the citizenship. It is reported that religious culture is a prominent contributing factor to marital stability. For those who would argue that it is inappropriate for the government of a secular society to support religion, it must be pointed out that a secular society does not have to be anti-religious, it only has to refrain from supporting one religion to the exclusion of others. Anti-religion is a commitment which is measurably unhelpful to the society as a whole. Supporting religions would be to the financial benefit of society as a whole.

Public policy and private life

Will utilitarians genuinely face the failure of their experiments and seek to ensure social well being? It is to be seriously doubted. Utilitarians have the other problem that the concept of the well-being of society includes the rights of individuals to choose to do what they like. Individual freedom is, indeed, part of the well-being of society. Yet when it is costing society billions of dollars each year, then individual freedoms should be matched by individual financial responsibilities. Why should the community as a whole have to foot the bill for some individuals' freedoms?

The social sexual revolution has effected our legislators and jurists to such an extent that they would not want to legislate morally against their own private desires. Utilitarianism, in effect, becomes an excuse for doing whatever we want to do.

Let us recall Bertrand Russell at this point. His recommendations about sexual morality were couched in terms of the general good of society—what needs to be done to make all people happier and their lives less burdensome. Yet we may consider Russell's own life when he wrote this. He was committed to a life of sexual immorality and used women for his own very selfish ends.[7] It so happens that in 1936 (when his essay on sexual ethics was published) he had just finished a long and very messy divorce from his second wife, Dora, in which he successfully fought to have their children made Wards of Chancery. The idea of no-fault divorce, after no more than a year of separation, must have seemed ideal to him. His suggestions may have been expressed as genuine wishes for the good of society, but can hardly be taken independently of his own very selfish desires for freedom from the ties of his marriage.

This has always been the problem with utilitarianism. It is not the real agenda. It is the intellectually respectable clothing for the choice to reject God and his ways. It is a rationalization for the immorality of doing whatever we want. Yet it is philosophically flawed and practically unworkable. Bertrand Russell was undoubtedly a very clever man. But clever men are very ingenious at rationalizing their wickedness.

Humans are limited, and although we may think our ethics are about increasing well-being, our horizons are generally much shorter. After all, whose well-being is it that matters the most? In personal terms, the utilitarian ethic is often reduced to the lowest denominator—we act in any way we want, unless it can be proven that such an action will hurt somebody else. When a person decides to fornicate or commit adultery, it will hardly be because of a general ideal that this will help society. Rather, the thought process—if there is one—is far more likely to be along the lines of: 'It feels right to me, and it's not hurting anyone, so why shouldn't I?'.

However, it is hurting someone. It is hurting all of us, and most of all those who live by permissiveness and their children. Until we have a reversal in society which realises the true importance of genuine morality and its basis in absolutes, our society will continue to pay. In the end, utilitarianism survives today only because there is no 'acceptable' alternative when God has been discounted. Having accepted a non-sectarian approach to society which has turned 'secular' into 'godless', there can now be no appeal to authority outside the government. There is no moral theory that the society will accept. To challenge utilitarianism is to challenge the working of our society. Yet utilitarianism has created a society which, in the most practical of terms, does not work. What Bible believers have predicted for generations is now a matter of free information. A social experiment was tried, the data proclaims that it has failed, and the philosophy on which our society is based has no idea what to do about it.

ENDNOTES

1 B. Russell, *Why I am Not a Christian and Other Essays on Religion and Related Subjects*, Unwin Books, London, 1967, p. 121.

2 *Ibid.*, p. 125.

3 Russell's essay is reproduced in B. Russell, *Why I am Not a Christian and Other Essays on Religion and Related Subjects*, pp. 120-127. The government report comes from the House of Representatives Standing Committee on Legal and Constitutional Affairs, June 1998. It can be obtained free of charge from Parliament House in Canberra, ACT, telephone (61 2) 6277 7222. Page references are to these documents.

4 Russell further saw the implications of the revolution: "It is clear, that, even where there are children, the State is only interested through the duties of fathers which are chiefly financial. Where divorce is easy, as in Scandinavia, the children usually go with the mother, so that the patriarchal family tends to disappear. If, as is increasingly happening where wage earners are concerned, the State takes over the duties that have hitherto fallen upon fathers, marriage will cease to have any *raison d'être*, and will probably be no longer customary except among the rich and the religious" (pp. 126-127).

5 B. Russell, *op. cit*, p. 126.

6 For an account of this development, see chapters 3 & 4 of T. Payne & P. D. Jensen, *Pure Sex*, Matthias Media, Sydney, 1997.

7 See 'Peace I did not find' on page 123 of this volume.

5.
Whose history of philosophy?

Jostein Gaarder
Sophie's World: A Novel about the History of Philosophy
Phoenix House, London, 1991.

*I*T'S THE SORT of story that publishers usually only dream of. A book, written by a little-known Scandinavian high-school teacher, about the history of Western philosophy of all things, became a run-away best-seller. In 1995, it sold over 8 million copies; a later count took it over 9 million. Defying all normal assumptions about academic topics, philosophy suddenly became hot property. Somehow, philosophy moved out of armchairs and ivory towers into the mainstream.

Sophie's World is subtitled 'A Novel about the History of Philosophy', which gives some indication of the point of the book. It is a novel—but more than that, it is an entertaining gallop through various chronologically-organized philosophical schools of thought. The reader ends up with an overview of Western philosophy, set in a novel in which the fictional characters work out their own drama in the light of these philosophical traditions.

Sophie's World is intriguing, both for what it says and for the fact of its popularity. The success of a book like *Sophie's World* must be an important sociological indicator of both intellectual desire and insecurity. For one, the idea of having within one novel the whole history of Western philosophy seems to be very attractive to the instant generation. Apart from the need to follow intellectual fashion, there is a sense that our education has omitted essential information about life and its meaning, and that the answer lies in the deep mysteries of philosophy. Here, then, is the chance to discover what the famous names actually taught.

There are other reasons why the popularity of this book is important. This is not a technical book but an educational apologetic for philosophy—and because it aims to be general, it tells us what 'general opinion' is. It is not seeking to present a particular slant on philosophy, or on its history, but trying to give the overview of what the discipline has been about and where it is up to now. Here is one of the 'summary of the consensus of scholarly opinion' books. As such, it is an indicator of the current status of our intellectual community.

Sophie's World is also striking if taken as representative of the mainstream intellectual view of philosophy. The book takes the intellectual high ground of the philosophers, singing the praises of genuine philosophy: critical, rational, and unbiased; removing prejudice, superstition and convention; not given to quick, rash judgments but relentlessly pursuing truth, knowledge, beauty and morality.

> And to be quite frank, that is precisely what we need philosophers for. We do not need them to choose a beauty queen or the day's bargain in tomatoes. (This is why they are unpopular!)

> Philosophers will try to ignore highly topical affairs and instead try to draw people's attention to what is eternally 'true', eternally 'beautiful', and eternally 'good' (pp. 65-6).

From this objective, eternal viewpoint, the book dismisses Christianity by domestication and association. While Christianity is given some prominence in the history, it is carefully placed in a negative category, as we will see. Yet it is significant that as the book draws to its close, philosophers also become strangely silent. The important thinkers for Gaarder are no longer philosophers in the generally understood sense, but Marx, Darwin, Freud and the researchers of modern astronomy. Knowledge is the result not of philosophers any more, but scientists. Is the discipline of philosophy, like Christianity, to be dismissed as a thing of the past?

The strengths

The author and the publishers deserve to be thanked for their efforts to make such important matters part of the common domain of social intercourse. This book enables those who love ideas and philosophy to share them with friends. It invites the wider community into the conversation of the great minds of the past.

The philosophy is clearly and simply written. Even when discussing obscure and abstract ideas, the writing never loses its clarity or accessibility. Few books will be able to open up philosophy to more people. The dust-jacket of the book tells us: "For eleven years, Jostein Gaarder taught philosophy in a high school in Bergen", and that experience obviously informs his approach to explaining philosophical concepts. Added to these advantages the novel format can involve the reader inside philosophical reasoning in a way that a more didactic book would not. Like any good teacher, Gaarder encourages revision by providing his characters with new reasons to reiterate the philosophical arguments. Those who have already read the book will recognize that the mid-novel plot twist, apart from being enjoyable, allows the reader to participate in a way that lifts the whole presentation.

As a novel alone, however, it is doubtful whether *Sophie's World* would deserve to be a success. The characters are fairly dull and uninteresting, the plot is thin, the conflict and tension are not particularly gripping, and there is a lack of real suspense. The whole story is just a little too unrealistic for the reader to care much what happens to the people involved. The characters are merely tools for the exposition of philosophy. The strange old man who is teaching Sophie philosophy never becomes anything other than a strange old man, and the precocious Sophie is never anything but a stooge of philosophical education. There is a certain juvenile directness to the style which may have been deliberate, for the sake of simplicity; but it does not make for a gripping read. (Maybe being in translation is part of the problem?)

The place of Christianity

One of the problems in recording the history of Western philosophy is the place that is going to be given to Christianity. Christianity has dominated

Western culture, and has an important interplay with philosophy both in antagonism and concurrence.

At first glance, *Sophie's World* is very positive towards Christianity. There are many references to it. Even when not specified, the God that is under discussion generally conforms to the Judeo-Christian God (though not necessarily the biblical, trinitarian God). Church plays a part in the lives of the characters and is used as scenery for some of the discussions. There is a chapter on Christ which shows more than a superficial understanding of his claims. There are repeated examples of the difference that holding a Christian view of God, especially as creator, would make. There are places where the misrepresentations of Christianity are corrected—for example the confusion that arose from the importation of Aristotelian views of women into the church. Luther is mentioned with some respect in the chapter on the Renaissance—there was more to him than just Indulgences. But none of the other Reformers appear, and Luther is only a part of the Renaissance, and a 'gloomy' part of it at that.

At second glance, the novel has a negative sub-text about Christianity. Philosophy, we are told, has had a long tradition of freeing people from the bonds of mythology, superstition and religion. Christianity is in the bondage side of the history, not the freedom side. It is true that most of the directly negative comments are levelled at the polytheistic ancient world religion or the modern New Age superstitions, rather than Christianity or in the possibility of God's existence—after all, some very respectable philosophers have argued for a non-materialistic philosophy. However, the philosopher of the book (Alberto) confesses to being a naturalist in the end (p. 360), and revelation as a source of knowledge is disparaged. Adam and Noah appear in the same place as Alice in Wonderland and Little Red Riding Hood, Jesus and his death are paralleled to Socrates and his death, and Christianity is an expression of the interaction of Semitic culture and Indo-European mythology. Science and philosophy are the judges of truth, not God or his word. Hilde's father works for the United Nations, the true bringers of peace in the world, especially in the religiously war-torn lands of the Middle East.

Despite the room it gives to Christianity, then, the novel fails to do justice to Christian views. The Trinitarian nature of Christianity does not fit into the simple philosophical question of the existence of God. To parallel Jesus' commitment to truth, and his death, to Socrates, is to misunderstand Jesus' teaching.[1]

The history of philosophy

Any book purporting to be about 'the history' of philosophy faces the problem of all histories; they are by necessity selective, and the more ground they try to cover the more selective they have to be.

The approach that selects a range of representative thinkers, rather than concentrating on just one school or topic, is the usual method of first-year university texts and courses. Without very much negative critique, all major views are outlined and given their due credit as significant contributions to the discipline. We do not adopt one view or another, but take on parts of all the truths that have been discovered. It is a useful approach for the beginner; it enables the newcomer to gain a grasp of the whole subject. It is also a safe approach for the writer. It has the appearance of objectivity, and by presenting all the main views evenhandedly, one demonstrates the important ability to appreciate others' viewpoints, and to represent them fairly.

Yet this kind of selectivity can have bad results, and cover unintended (or intended) biases. Its impression of objectivity is deceptive. The gathering of certain great thinkers into a book does not give a history of great thinkers, but a collection. In the collection, decisions of whom to include and whom to exclude involve the value judgements and biases of the collector. Yet by having a sufficiently large collection, by being polite about everyone and by including people that you really do not agree with, it is possible to convey the idea of some objectivity—and it enables the author to avoid making a decision and arguing a case.

In this novel, the philosophy that Jostein Gaarder is interested in is not that of logic, mathematics or semantics. Moore, Russell, Wittgenstein, Popper and Ayer are not given any place as the story diverts to Marx, Freud, Darwin and cosmology. Certain topics continue to appear whether or not they were the concerns of philosophers, for this is a very politically correct novel. All the modern shibboleths are mentioned: ecology, feminism, tolerance, Eastern religion, comparative religion, the UN and the new world order. This may be to make the issue of philosophy relevant to today, or to include the readers from as wide an audience as possible, but mostly it seems to be because these issues are the ones that matter to the author.

Here is not 'A Novel about the History of Philosophy', but an eclectic look at some of the philosophical roots of a modern naturalistic humanism. In the end, science is deferred to as the adjudicator of truth, and materialism, while not dogmatically certain, is definitely the preferred option. However, while we are led to these conclusions, we are not actually given the reasons for them. We have an impression that this is where the combined wisdom of the ages will lead us; but a different history would have led us to a different end-point.

Questions for Sophie

This book is no marginal work. It presents itself as a general, mainstream history of philosophy, and its popularity demonstrates that it fits such a niche. As such, it claims moral and intellectual superiority over other views (such as Christianity) but does not present a compelling case for this superiority. Its conclusions are little more than its assumptions, and many of these assumptions could do with more examination.

For one, the anti-God nature of the assumptions is not analysed philosophically. The Christian objections to naturalism are not even mentioned, while the victories of Socrates over the religiously superstitious and of the materialists over the Platonists are expounded clearly. Another unexplored assumption is the reality of meaning and the value of philosophical investigation. Even though as the novel progresses the world is presented as a great accident, it is not to be viewed as meaningless. Sophie, it seems, must find meaning in the world's excitement or its immensity or its wonder. Yet she does not ask the questions of how one *can* find meaning in an accident.

Displaying another unexamined assumption, especially on politically correct issues, the writer commends ethical and civilized behaviour. Yet the reader is never given any basis for ethical or civilized behaviour. Christians have a clearly explained basis for such behaviour in the character and purposes of our creator and saviour. We even understand why it is that people who reject God will continue upholding ethical standards, for they are made by him whether or not they acknowledge him. The non-Christian view presented in this book, on the other hand, prides itself on the rigour of its intellectual inquiry but gives few reasons for the behaviour and ethics it is commending (so at this point, at least, has little ground for rejecting Christianity). The book does not teach the acceptance of Kantian ethics, nor the rejection of Neitzsche's ethics, but gives a quick nod to both and encourages us to find our own. The same problem can be seen on the question of knowledge. While certain forms of knowledge such as the New Age and religious superstition are rejected, there is no real explanation of the writer's view of knowledge—just the assurance that physicists now know.[2] Science is not challenged to show its philosophical basis. There is just a utilitarian bowing to the success of science—it works, therefore it is true.

Sophie's World leaves us asking questions—the questions that have been left unanswered by this look at philosophy. We are left feeling at the end of *Sophie's World* that after the effort of centuries of thinking, we know little more than when we started. This has to make one wonder—if the great minds cannot come to any answer, what is wrong? Is it just possible that there is a flaw in the assumption that we by ourselves are able and capable from our 'unbiased' viewpoint, unaided by any revelation of our maker, to come to an understanding of the true nature of the human condition?

I am reminded of the teachings of Ecclesiastes.

> I have seen the burden God has laid on men. He has made everything beautiful in its time. He has also set eternity in the hearts of men; yet they cannot fathom what God has done from beginning to end (Eccl 3:10-11).

ENDNOTES

1   Gaarder has a generally good understanding of the New Testament; it is just unfortunate that at the point of Jesus' death he has some crucial misplaced emphases. It is true that both Jesus and Socrates died "for the sake of their convictions" (p. 52)—but more importantly Jesus died for the sin of mankind. "[B]y meeting their death so bravely they commanded an enormous following, also after they had died" (p. 53)—however Jesus is not followed because of his courage, but because he died for the sin of the whole world. Moreover Socrates' teaching would be true or false independently of his death, while without the

death of Jesus the whole of his teaching fails completely.
2   Scientists are the rule by which knowledge is tested, in Gaarder's view. "Democritus *believed* that nature consisted of an unlimited number and variety of atoms" but "Today we can *establish* that Democritus' atom theory was more or less correct" (p. 35). "In Darwin's time, it was widely *believed* that about 6,000 years had elapsed since God created the earth" but "... today we *know* that the earth is 4.6 billion year old" (my italics), p. 315.

6.
Peace I did not find

Ray Monk
Bertrand Russell: The Spirit of Solitude
Jonathan Cape, London, 1996.

$\mathcal{B}$ERTRAND RUSSELL contributed greatly to the Christian cause by giving generations of preachers quotable quotes from his *Why I am not a Christian*. His work in the foundations of mathematics forms a standard part of many a philosophy and mathematics course. He was famous in his lifetime for his philosophy, his political views, his outspoken opposition to World War I, and his opposition to Christianity. He was one of the shapers of thought and society in this century, and so his biography deserves attention from all those who would understand modern life, if for no other reason than that in his own life, Russell lived out the consequences of the desperately pessimistic atheism which he preached.

That he did so, however, was little known at the time. While Russell was seen as the hero of non-Christian morality—he did, after all, resist war and fight for women's rights—his own lifestyle was a vast travesty of morality, but public recognition of this was suppressed. It is telling that the biography written during Russell's lifetime, with Russell's help, had little personal detail, which Monk puts down both to lack of means (as that biographer did not have access to Russell's unpublished work) as well as lack of inclination. Russell was, to put it baldly, a hypocrite. Now that society has changed so that revealing sordid details of personal immorality does not destroy a person's reputation, the story can be told. One wonders what the effect would have been had it been told during the time his views were becoming so influential. It would most likely have destroyed his public reputation. Russell's personal life was no great advertisement for this man who stood as a moralist, a crusader for sexual reform, and a public enemy of Christianity.

This massive beginning to the biography of Bertrand Russell is an impressive piece of work. It is well written, but not easy to read casually, as its meticulous detail swamps any story line. This is (apparently) deliberate: the author tries to give us enough of Russell's own words to understand the man first-hand. Russell wrote voluminously, thousands of words each day, many in letters that he and others have preserved. There is a mountain of self-absorbed writing available on Russell's almost-daily doings. This makes the work more a chronicle than a biography; what it tries to show of Russell's character could have been accomplished in considerably less space. However, if the author is trying to give the definitive reference to which all future Russell studies can refer, he has certainly provided a wealth of material. In 612 pages of text and 73 pages of notes, references and index, the biographer has only covered the period 1872-1921.

One of the strengths of this book is its pursuit of Russell's philosophical development and reasoning. Russell's claim to fame was as a philosopher, and to show little interest in this area would be to seriously distort our understanding of him. He was also a man of some social and political importance in his lifetime. He was introduced to Queen Victoria, spent an hour with Lenin, lectured to Mao, knew Prime Ministers personally, and lectured in the leading universities of the world. It is a life worth telling.

However, the book is not just a description of philosophy. It truly tries to understand the man from the events of his life. To do such a task well, there needs to be some intellectual accord between the writer and the reader about the nature of the man himself. It also depends upon the writer's understanding of human nature. As regards the former, this book is a success, with its careful documentation. As regards the latter, it is striking how well Russell illustrates the Christian understanding of the nature of man, and the nature of sin and its consequences. Monk has no such perspective, however, and so avenues for understanding Russell which are obvious to a Christian mind are left out entirely. This is illustrated in the biographer's failure to search out connections between the morality and philosophy of the philosopher, except in some vague psychological categories. It is also seen in the omission of reference to the kind of Christianity that Russell came into contact with. The author considers that Russell's character was strongly shaped by the way in which he reacted against his pious grandmother while still seeking her approval, but there is no discussion of the particular nature of her piety—for instance, the fact that she was not an orthodox Christian, but Unitarian.

The thesis of the biography is that Russell was right when he said of himself that there were three passions that ruled his life: "the longing for love, the search for knowledge, and the unbearable pity for the suffering of mankind" (xviii). However to understand these three passions and their conflict with each other, it is necessary to understand that they were alternative answers to the same single problem that really dominated him: "the problem of his acute sense of isolation and loneliness, a problem that was for him compounded by his extraordinarily deep-seated fear of madness" (xix). The author quotes a poem of Russell's, which begins:

> Through the long years
> I sought peace,
> I found ecstasy, I found anguish,
> I found madness,
> I found loneliness.
> I found the solitary pain that gnaws the heart,
> But peace I did not find (quoted p. xix).

This, we take it, sums up Russell's life.

Maybe to the reader's surprise, this is not a secular hagiography; it has too much contact with the source material. The author states:

> I am aware that the personality thus revealed is one that many will find repellent, but it has not

been my aim to present him in an unfavourable
light. There are many things for which I admire
Russell greatly—his enormous intelligence, his
commitment to social justice and international
peace, and so on. But the challenge to those of us
who admire him is to understand how they can
coexist with a sometimes quite chilling coldness
to those close to him, and a disturbing capacity
for deep and dark hatreds (xix-xx).

It is difficult to know what more to say of this book as a biography, given that it is only the first volume; it finishes with Russell aged 49 (he died at the age of 98). We wait for the second volume to see how the author completes his understanding of Russell's life.[1] Nevertheless, enough of Russell's character is presented to provide an illuminating example of a man struggling against despair. In many ways Russell is the picture of the intellectual who has discarded the Christian world view—which he deliberately rejected—and lives out the consequences.

Russell the person, as revealed in this book, is almost horrifying. Those who know him only as a philosopher, or even as the author of *Why I am not a Christian*, will probably recoil at the details of his personal life. Whatever pity we feel for Russell's internal struggles and desperation is countered by the suffering he inflicted upon those around him. At times Russell showed a twisted honesty in recognizing the implications of what he believed, and deliberately mistreating others as a result. At other times he seems to be hideous in his self-deception. Either way he is a chilling example of the deliberately godless life.

Russell's romantic relationships make rather sordid telling. He married at the age of 22, desperate for a sexual relationship. It was a self-centred reason for marriage; he did not love his wife for herself (in fact by the time of his marriage he had let his wife know he was considerably attracted to her sister) but for his own benefit. When she no longer suited him he "fell out of love" with her. This led to years of an almost double life, as the Russells developed a strange relationship with Alfred North Whitehead and his wife, Evelyn. Russell allowed himself to fall in love with Evelyn Whitehead, who would not accept his advances, but he continued in unfulfilled passion for her for years, while working with, and being friends, with her husband.

The story has many strange episodes, which philosophy students studying the work of Russell and Whitehead would no doubt be surprised to hear. In 1901, Bertrand and his wife, Alys, moved in temporarily with the Whiteheads in Cambridge. While there, during the time that Whitehead's wife was very ill, Bertrand went through what he called his 'first conversion'; he was "filled with semi-mystical feelings about beauty, with an intense interest in children, and a desire almost as profound as that of the buddha to find some philosophy which should make human life endurable" (p. 135). He said this brought him closer to other people, something that enabled him to feel other people's suffering. However as the biographer says, "there was at least one person to whose suffering he became extraordinarily blind and indifferent after this experience, and that was Alys" (p. 138). Because of Evelyn's illness, she was expected to take over the running of the household and the care of the Whitehead's children. A close friend described Bertrand at the time as without sympathy and tolerance for other people's emotions, even though these were the very things that Russell considered he had acquired through his conversion experience (p. 139).

Following this, however, Russell developed a bizarre philosophy based on the idea that dishonesty was the root of all evil and honesty the basis of all virtue. Since the highest good consisted in contemplating the truth, and truth cannot be achieved without pain and suffering, therefore to cause suffering was virtuous (p. 154). Russell put this into practice by deliberately causing his wife emotional pain and treating her with chilling indifference. Although he later repented of this and decided it was better to treat Alys decently, his bleak view of humanity remained. His only solace was mathematics. He saw mathematics as sublime, the

> chief means of overcoming the terrible sense of impotence, of weakness, or exile amid hostile powers, which is too apt to result from acknowledging the all-but omnipotence of alien forces ... mathematics takes us still further from what is human, into the realm of absolute necessity (p. 159).

It was desirable to escape from what is human. The man who wrote "Whatever knowledge is attainable, must be attained by scientific methods; and what science cannot discover, mankind cannot know"[2] also thought "the world which Science presents for our belief is entirely purposeless and indifferent to the hopes and the sufferings of mankind" (pp. 162-3).

Russell's first adulterous relationship was with Ottoline Morrell, wife of a political friend of Russell's. His life thereafter was to include a string of (often simultaneous) relationships, in which he lied to his lovers, made promises which he later ignored, and seemed generally indifferent to anyone's feelings but his own. After having been separated from Alys for several years, Russell admitted what he really wanted was a wife. "Since I quarrelled with Alys", he wrote in a letter to his lover Ottoline, "I have never found any one who would or could take me away for holidays when I am tired or take care of me and now I find without something of the kind I am no good" (p. 543). He was in an emotionally drained state, it seems, having just helped another lover, Colette, get an abortion (which at this time was illegal) for a pregnancy from another man. The relationship that eventually led to marriage was not long in coming; he met twenty-five-year-old Dora Black, and began an affair at this time, although his correspondence with Colette still insisted he loved her more than ever and she could trust him utterly (p. 557).

Russell's self-centredness in his conduct of these affairs, his deceit and hypocrisy, is breathtaking. His treatment of the young American woman Helen Dudley can only be described as inhuman degeneracy—and from the man who claimed to be the first to stand for parliament for women's rights. He met Helen while travelling in America, and suggested she come back to live with him in England, eventually to get married if he could get a divorce from Alys. At the same time, he told Ottoline that he had slept with Helen only out of philanthropy, to foster her creativeness as a writer (p. 356). After a few days back in England, Russell decided that the relationship with Helen was not so serious after all, particularly since Ottoline was not at all happy about it. When Helen arrived in England—having no idea of his change of heart—Russell refused even to see her. The biographer is able to show by a careful study of the correspondence that Russell's own account of the affair in his autobiography is totally hypocritical. Her final state—in an asylum—is pathos itself. Another one of Russell's lovers to end in an asylum was (the married) Vivien Eliot. The biographer seems to have no sympathy for Russell on this issue, and seems to believe the worst about Russell's responsibility for her final incarceration. Russell lied about the extent of the affair, disowned responsibility, and claimed to be helping the Eliots' marriage by allowing Vivien to fall in love with him.

Russell was, in fact, an inveterate liar. He developed lying as a technique in his youth to protect himself from his grandmother, and used it consistently in his marriage, in the conduct of his tangled relationships, and in his professional affairs (e.g. p. 572).

✠

It is Russell's treatment of people which is most disturbing, but other areas of his character also reveal a confusing personality. It is interesting to find that Russell was not a pacifist, even though he opposed World War I, to the extent of going to prison as a conscientious objector. He did not, however, oppose war as such. His opposition to that war had to do with friendship with Ludwig Wittgenstein and Joseph Conrad, love of German culture, and dislike of Russia, the pointless destruction of civilization, and the diplomatic avoidability of the conflict. Russell approved of colonial wars such as those against Maoris and Aborigines (p. 383), where the purpose and effect were (he thought) civilizing.

Russell was anti-Semitic, and considerably racist in his expressions of national and personal snobbery. "I find the coloured people friendly and nice", he wrote to Ottoline from America, "They seem to have something of a dog's liking for the white man" (p. 348). He had a very dark side to his nature, twice trying to murder somebody—once his poor wife Alys, the other time his friend Edward Fitzgerald. He worried over the dark side of his nature, and his writings do talk of religion, sin and guilt. He likened himself to "the sinister embittered murderer" Rogojin in Dostoyevsky's *The Idiot*.

✣

Throughout this strange life, it is interesting to see Russell's views on the importance of religion. He had an understanding of universal sinfulness—he hated pacifists "who keep saying human nature is essentially good, in spite of all the daily proofs to the contrary" (p. 490), and agreed with Jeremiah 17:9 that "the heart is deceitful above all things, and desperately wicked: who can know it?" which Russell said was "Freud in a nutshell" (p. 536).

More than that, Russell saw an importance in the ideas of religion or eternity. "If life is to be fully human", he wrote, "it must serve some end which seems, in some sense, outside human life, some end which is impersonal and above mankind, such as God or truth or beauty" (p. 447). In other words, "Those who best promote life do not have life for their purpose ..." (p. 447). These views emphasize the way in which Russell was a living contradiction, a tension he felt himself. He rejected the pursuit of happiness (p. 446), and saw the benefits of religion and many of its truths; but he was an atheist, trying to live in a world of mathematical certainty, whose certainty his own philosophy had undermined.

Russell searched for meaning, which continually eluded him, and tried to escape the solitude of his own thoughts. "I care passionately for this world and many things and people in it, and yet ... what is it all?" he wrote from prison. "There *must* be something more important, one feels, though I don't *believe there* is" (p. 530). Like the writer of Ecclesiastes, he could see that although he did not know God, the experience of life demanded and required there to be a God. For Russell, human affection "is to me at bottom an attempt to escape from the vain search for God" (p. 531). At the same time, he desired intensely to depersonalize everything, to live with the abstract, not limited by particulars. This may have been the root of his hatred of mankind:

> ... it is the human race that is vile. It is a disgrace to belong to it. Being busy is like taking opium, it enables one to live in a land of golden dreams— I must get busy again. The truth is not the sort of thing one can live with (p. 490).

This volume of the biography ends with Russell just having become a father. It closes on a hopeful and yet ominous note:

> In their various ways, his early religious beliefs, his belief in the platonic realm of mathematics, his faith in revolutionary socialism and even the ecstasies of romantic love had all disappointed him; they had all turned out to be mere 'phantoms in the dusk', disappearing in the cold light of day. But fatherhood, the binding love and loyalty (as Conrad put it) between a man and his son—that, surely, was as real as any contact can be between one person and another. And in that contact, equally surely, Russell thought, he would find the lasting release from the prison of the self, from the feeling of being a 'ghost', for which he had longed all his life (p. 612).

A tormented and lonely human, Russell treated others with inhumanity. As such, Russell is an illustration— almost a self-acknowledged one—of the hopelessness and immorality of atheism. He was famous for his philosophy and his liberalism, his championing of women's rights and his opposition to World War I. However, the public face of the hero could not be more contradicted by the life of the person. This person who stands as such a major figure in modern philosophy is hardly a positive advertisement of the practical worth of his own views. It is easy to shy away from telling such stories, for they make unsavoury reading. In telling the story of his life, however, the point is not merely to repeat scandalous stories, but to bring to the surface the hopelessness that stems from the views. Ideas have consequences in real life; Bertrand Russell is a sad example of this.

ENDNOTES
1   The second volume has now been published; the picture it draws of Bertrand Russell in later life is not substantially different.
2   Bertrand Russell, *Religion and Science*, Oxford University Press, London, 1935.

matthiasmedia

Matthias Media is an independent, evangelical, non-denominational company based in Sydney, Australia. We produce an extensive range of Bible studies, books, Bible reading materials, evangelistic tools, training resources, periodicals and multimedia resources. In all that we do, our mission is:

To serve our Lord Jesus Christ, and the growth of his gospel in Australia and the world, by producing and delivering high quality, Bible-based resources.

For more information about our resources, and to browse our online catalogue, visit our website at **www.matthiasmedia.com.au**. (US customers may visit: www.matthiasmedia.com. In the UK and Europe, our resources are distributed by The Good Book Company at www.thegoodbook.co.uk.)

You can also contact us in any of the following ways:

Mail:	Matthias Media PO Box 225 Kingsford NSW 2032 Australia
Telephone:	1800 814 360 *(tollfree in Australia)* 9663 1478 *(in Sydney)* +61 2 9663 1478 *(international)*
Facsimile:	9663 3265 *(in Sydney)* +61 2 9663 3265 *(international)*
Email:	info@matthiasmedia.com.au

The Myths of Science

When Christianity is mentioned in the context of science or modern knowledge, a few old pennies will inevitably turn up: church persecution of scientists such as Galileo and Giordano Bruno, David Hume's refutation of miracles, Darwin's defeat of the biblical view of creation, the Scopes 'monkey trial' which showed up fundamentalism as foolish. These myths are not true, but appear regularly on television and in all sorts of publications. *Myths of Science* presents *kategoria* essays on these topics, to prove that the old stories that pit Christianity against science may still be circulating, but are still wrong.

READER REVIEW: "Kirsten Birkett's scriptural soundness, matched with her insight, research and clarity of expression, make her books a joy to read."

Clare Booth Steward, *Christian Woman Magazine*

FOR MORE INFORMATION CONTACT:

Australia
Matthias Media
Telephone: +61-2-9663 1478
Facsimile: +61 2-9663 3256
Email: sales@matthiasmedia.com.au

United Kingdom
The Good Book Company
Telephone: 0845-225-0880
Facsimile: 0845-225-0990
Email: admin@thegoodbook.co.uk

www.matthiasmedia.com.au

Pure Sex

Phillip Jensen and Tony Payne take a look at what the Bible teaches about sex, and at what this means in the sexual climate of the new millennium. In doing so, they give Christians clear and compelling reasons for standing apart and being different from the world around them; but they also provide a challenge to the non-Christian person who realises that something is very wrong with the model of sexuality we are now living with, post the sexual revolution.

This compelling book shows how our society has come to hold such a confused and destructive view of sex, and why the Bible's alternative is so liberating.

FOR MORE INFORMATION CONTACT:

Australia
Matthias Media
Telephone: +61-2-9663 1478
Facsimile: +61 2-9663 3256
Email: sales@matthiasmedia.com.au

United Kingdom
The Good Book Company
Telephone: 0845-225-0880
Facsimile: 0845-225-0990
Email: admin@thegoodbook.co.uk

www.matthiasmedia.com.au

Islam in our Backyard

WINNER
AUSTRALIAN CHRISTIAN BOOK OF THE YEAR 2003

The events of September 11 catapulted Islam back into Western consciousness. Was this the opening shot in a new level of conflict between the 'Islamic' East and the 'Christian' West? How much were the attacks bound up with Islam itself? Just what does Islam teach, and how are we in the West to relate to it?

In this unique book—part novel, part essay—Tony Payne explores these questions via a series of conversations with his fictional neighbour, Michael. He goes behind the media stereotypes to examine the beliefs and teachings of Islam, in their essence and in their diversity, and explains the origins of Islamic radical groups like the Taliban.

More than that, he explores the religious challenge that Islam brings to Western society—not just in relation to terrorism, but in how we are going to deal with the big questions of 'God' and 'truth' in a multicultural society.

FOR MORE INFORMATION CONTACT:

Australia
Matthias Media
Telephone: +61-2-9663 1478
Facsimile: +61 2-9663 3256
Email: sales@matthiasmedia.com.au

United Kingdom
The Good Book Company
Telephone: 0845-225-0880
Facsimile: 0845-225-0990
Email: admin@thegoodbook.co.uk

www.matthiasmedia.com.au

Unnatural Enemies

"History records that whenever science and orthodoxy have been fairly opposed, the latter has been forced to retire from the lists, bleeding and crushed, if not annihilated; scotched if not slain." So argued Thomas Huxley, one of the nineteenth century's great champions of science against Christian belief.

Was he right? Are science and Christianity destined to be bitter enemies? Is it possible to be a Christian and a good scientist?

In this compellingly readable introduction to the subject, Kirsten Birkett looks at both science and Christianity, clearly explaining what both are about, and dispelling many common confusions and misunderstandings. She argues that while there are no necessary grounds for the two to be at war, there is still reason to think that the conflict might continue.

For all interested in science—Christian or non-Christian, professional, student or lay—Dr Birkett's perspective as both a Christian and an historian of science sheds new light on these perennial questions.

FOR MORE INFORMATION CONTACT:

Australia
Matthias Media
Telephone: +61-2-9663 1478
Facsimile: +61 2-9663 3256
Email: sales@matthiasmedia.com.au

United Kingdom
The Good Book Company
Telephone: 0845-225-0880
Facsimile: 0845-225-0990
Email: admin@thegoodbook.co.uk

www.matthiasmedia.com.au

The Essence of Darwinism

Is Darwinism true? Is it the only theory that can explain our origins? Should we care? Are we taking Genesis seriously enough?

In her fourth book in *The Essence of* series, Dr Kirsten Birkett considers these frequently asked questions. In an area in which there seem to be so many conflicting answers, she takes a fresh look at the controversy by getting behind the surface disputes to look at what is really being argued over. At the same time, this book provides a compact and accessible summary of the important points of the Darwinian theory so far.

The Essence of Darwinism is an easy-to-read book for all thinkers from senior high school onwards.

FOR MORE INFORMATION CONTACT:

Australia
Matthias Media
Telephone: +61-2-9663 1478
Facsimile: +61 2-9663 3256
Email: sales@matthiasmedia.com.au

United Kingdom
The Good Book Company
Telephone: 0845-225-0880
Facsimile: 0845-225-0990
Email: admin@thegoodbook.co.uk

www.matthiasmedia.com.au

The Essence of Feminism

Feminism has permeated the modern world—it affects how we act, how we think, how we speak. It is one of the most powerful forces in Western society. How did it get to be that way? Are its claims true and are its arguments valid?

In this book, Kirsten Birkett has researched the origins of modern feminism, what it fought for and what it has achieved. She began writing the book considering herself a feminist. By the end, she was no longer one and this book explains why.

The Essence of Feminism is certain to challenge and educate its readers. It is required reading for anyone seeking to understand and respond to the most significant social movement of our generation.

FOR MORE INFORMATION CONTACT:

Australia
Matthias Media
Telephone: +61-2-9663 1478
Facsimile: +61 2-9663 3256
Email: sales@matthiasmedia.com.au

United Kingdom
The Good Book Company
Telephone: 0845-225-0880
Facsimile: 0845-225-0990
Email: admin@thegoodbook.co.uk

www.matthiasmedia.com.au